Alina Wheeler

Designing Brand Identity

A Complete Guide to Creating, Building, and Maintaining Strong Brands

WILEY

John Wiley & Sons, Inc.

Cover brand identity credits are listed left to right, starting at top.

Sanctum: Frankfurt Balkind

Brooklyn Academy of Music: Pentagram

Pharmacia:
 Logo, Landor Associates
 Program, Crosby Associates

Zoom: WGBH Boston

Chase Manhattan: Chermayeff & Geismar

FedEx: Landor Associates

Bank of America: Enterprise IG

Center City District: Joel Katz Design Associates

Cingular Wireless: VSA Partners

Tate: Wolff Olins

BP: Landor Associates

Chicago GSB: Crosby Associates

Intersection: Rev Group

Citi:
 Logo, Pentagram
 Signage, Lippincott & Margulies

The Franklin Institute Science Museum: Allemann, Almquist & Jones

Published by John Wiley & Sons, Inc., Hoboken, New Jersey
Published simultaneously in Canada

Library of Congress Cataloging-in-Publication Data:

Wheeler, Alina.
    Designing brand identity : a complete guide to creating, building, and maintaining
        strong brands / Alina Wheeler.
      p. cm.
    Includes bibliographical references and index.
    ISBN 0-471-21326-8 (pbk.)
    1. Brand name products. 2. Brand name products—Marketing—Management. 3.
    Trademarks—Design. 4. Advertising—Brand name products. I. Title.

HD69.B7 W44 2003
658.8′27—dc21

2002033142

Printed in the United States of America

10 9 8 7 6 5 4 3 2

Thank you to all the
individuals who took the time
to share their wisdom.

Lissa Reidel
Bart Crosby
Joel Katz
Steff Geissbuhler
Chris Pullman
Paula Scher
Michael Bierut
Dana Arnett
Jack Summerford
Tom Geismar
Woody Pirtle
Milton Glaser
Clay Timon
Gael Towey
Stephen Doyle
Janice Fudyma
Craig Bernhardt
Brian Tierney
Margie Gorman
Malcolm Grear
Emily Cohen
Jamie Koval
Andrew Welsh
Hans-U. Alleman
Steve Sandstrom
Aubrey Balkind
Kent Hunter
Sean Adams
Peter Wise
Richard Saul Wurman
Stella Gassaway
Margaret Anderson
Ivan Chermayeff
Doug Wolfe
Louise Fili
Heidi Cody
Le Roux Jooste
Sylvia Harris
Gerry Stankus
Jerry Selber
Russ Napolitano
Steve Perry
Joanne Chan
Bonita Albertson
Meredith Nierman
Betty Nelson
Pat Baldridge

Dr. Dennis Dunn
Bob Mueller
Jack Cassidy
Tom Watson
Bruce Berkowitz
Richard Kauffman
Pat Duci
Jaeho Ko
Lee Soonmee
Steve Storti
Sally Hudson
Erich Sippel
Hilary Jay
Geoff Verney
Trish Thompson
Dr. Virginia Vanderslice
Dr. Karol Wasylyshyn
Marilyn Sifford
Bobbi Jacobs-Meadway
Melissa Lapid
John Kerr
Helen Keyes
Richard Cress
Ned Drew
Mark Wills
Amy Grove-Bigham
Matthew Bartholomew
Deborah Perloe

Appreciation
John Wiley & Sons, Inc.
Margaret Cummins, editor
Diana Cisek, managing editor
Rosanne Koneval

Gratitude in perpetuity
Suzanne Young, editor
Meejoo Kwon, designer
Mary Storm-Baranyai,
production
Heather Norcini

Special mention to my brother
who asked when the film
is coming out

Deepest affection
Eddy Wheeler
Tessa Wheeler
Tearson Wheeler
Aiden Morrison
Sullivan

1
Perception

Part 1 defines the difference between brand and brand identity, and what it takes to be the best. A set of fundamental concepts forms the foundation of a successful brand identity process. It holds true regardless of the size and nature of the client or the scope of the project.

This book is one-stop learning about brand identity. It's an accessible resource that provides a road map to the process, explains some fundamental concepts, and showcases best practices. In the heat of a big project, it's easy to forget these core concepts; then again, maybe we never quite understood them and didn't want to ask. This resource supports a larger goal: to create, build, and manage strong brands, and to demonstrate why brand identity is a vital investment in the future.

All subject matter is organized by spread for easy accessibility.

Author's note

Brand identity implies an asset. Corporate identity sounds too much like an expense. I think this is an important distinction.

2
Process

Part 2 presents the brand identity process. The process underlies all successful brand identity work, regardless of the nature and size of the project. This section answers the question "Why does it take so long?"

3
Practice

Part 3 presents a series of case studies that reflect best practices. From local to global, from public through private, the range is a spectrum of branding and brand identity projects created by firms with diverse methodologies and strengths—from branding and design consultancies to in-house departments.

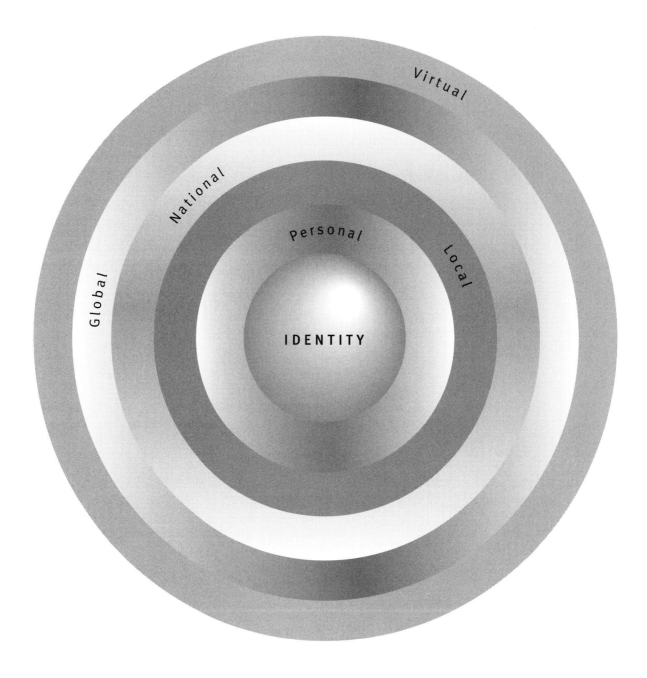

Global

National

Virtual

Personal

Local

IDENTITY

Since the beginning of time, the need to communicate emerges from a set of universal questions: Who am I? Who needs to know? Why do they need to know? How will they find out? How do I want them to respond? Individuals, communities, and organizations express their individuality through their identity. On the continuum from the cave paintings at Lascaux to digital messages transmitted via satellite, humanity continues to create an infinite sensory palette of visual and verbal expression.

Mankind has always used symbols to express fierce individuality, pride, loyalty, and ownership. The power of symbols remains elusive and mysterious—a simple form can instantaneously trigger recall and arouse emotion, whether it is emblazoned on a flag, etched in stone, or embedded in an e-mail. The velocity of life in the future will demand that brands, more than ever, leverage the power of symbols.

Competition for recognition is as ancient as the heraldic banners on a medieval battlefield. No longer limited by physical terrain, managing perception now extends to cyberspace and beyond. As feudal domains became economic enterprises, what was once heraldry is now branding. The battle for physical territory has evolved into the competition for share of mind.

Brand is the promise, the big idea, and expectations that reside in each customer's mind about a product, service or company. Branding is about making an emotional connection. People fall in love with brands—they trust them, develop strong loyalties, buy them, and believe in their superiority. The brand is shorthand: it stands for something and demonstrates it.

Branding used to be the exclusive purview of big consumer products. Now every business talks about the brand imperative, and even individuals are challenged by Tom Peters to become walking brands. Why have brands become so important? Bottom line: good brands build companies. Ineffective brands undermine success. As products and services become indistinguishable, as competition creates infinite choices, as companies merge into faceless monoliths, differentiation is imperative.

While being remembered is essential, it's becoming harder every day. A strong brand stands out in a densely crowded marketplace. Translating the brand into action has become an employee mantra. There is substantial evidence that companies whose employees understand and embrace the brand are more successful. What began as corporate culture under the auspices of human resources is fast becoming branding, and the marketing department runs the show.

Products are created in the factory. Brands are created in the mind.

Walter Landor, founder, Landor Associates

Brand has entered everyone's lexicon. The term is a chameleon—meaning can change with context. Sometimes it's a noun, as in "That's my brand of choice," and sometimes a verb, as in "Let's brand this campaign." It's become synonymous with the name of the company and its reputation.

Brands are embedded in our daily lives, as in "Let's FedEx it to Chattanooga" or "Just do it." The work of Andy Warhol and Heidi Cody remind us of the omnipresent power of brands as cultural symbols. For many, the brand is the trademark. Even those who don't precisely know what a brand is want one.

Brand Touchpoints

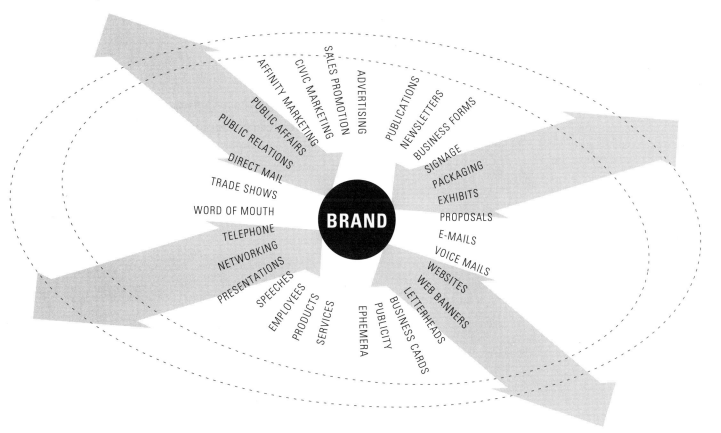

Each touchpoint is an opportunity to strengthen a brand and to communicate about its essence.

The brand is the nucleus of sales and marketing activities which result in increased awareness and loyalty when managed strategically.

While brands speak to the mind and heart, brand identity is tangible and appeals to the senses. Brand identity is the visual and verbal expression of a brand. Identity supports, expresses, communicates, synthesizes, and visualizes the brand. It is the shortest, fastest, most ubiquitous form of communication available. You can see it, touch it, hold it, hear it, watch it move. It begins with a brand name and a brandmark and builds exponentially into a matrix of tools and communications. On applications from business cards to websites, from advertising campaigns to fleets of planes and signage, brand identity increases awareness and builds businesses.

A logo is the point of entry to the brand.

Milton Glaser, designer

From the left to right

Bank of America:
Enterprise IG

BP: Landor Associates

Chase Manhattan:
Chermayeff & Geisimar

Foodsource:
Bonita Albertson

Zoom:
WGBH Boston

American Folk Art Museum:
Pentagram

The Franklin Institute:
Allemann, Almquist & Jones

Sanctum:
Frankfurt Balkind

Tate:
Wolff Olins

PowerBook G4:
Apple Computer

Intersection:
Rev Group

Center City District:
Joel Katz Design Associates

Cingular Wireless:
VSA Partners

Brooklyn Academy of Music:
Pentagram

Citigroup:
Pentagram

Solow Building Company:
Chermayeff & Geisimar

FedEx:
Landor Associates

Amazon.com:
Turner Duckworth

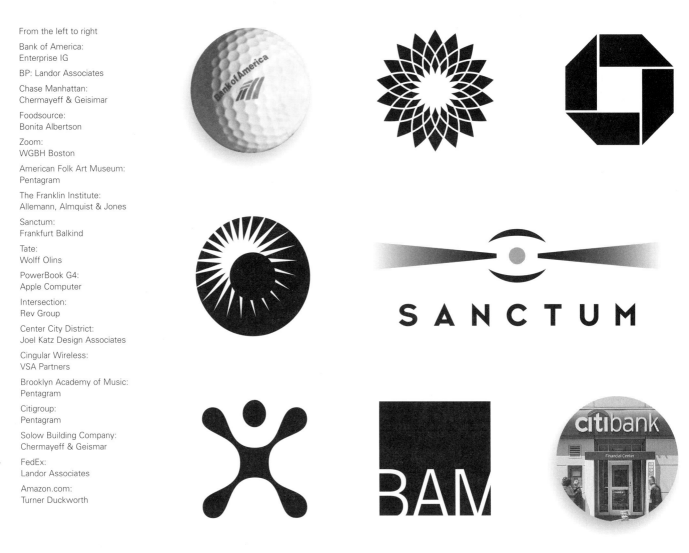

The need for effective brand identity cuts across public and private sectors, from new companies to merged organizations to businesses that need to reposition or repackage themselves. The best brand identity systems are memorable, authentic, meaningful, differentiated, sustainable, flexible, and have value. Recognition becomes immediate across cultures and customs.

Brand identity is a tool that is powerful and ubiquitous. Brand identity is an asset that needs to be managed, nourished, invested in, and leveraged. Done well, it is the consistent reminder of the meaning of the brand.

Building awareness and recognition of a brand is facilitated by a visual identity that is easy to remember and immediately recognizable. Visual identity triggers perceptions and unlocks associations of the brand. Vision, more than any other sense, provides a person with information about the world. Through repeated exposure of certain brand identities, symbols become so recognizable that companies such as Apple, Nike, and Merrill Lynch have actually dropped the logotype from their corporate signatures in national advertising. Color becomes a mnemonic device—when you see a brown truck out of the corner of your eye, you know it's UPS.

Identity designers are in the business of managing perception through the integration of meaning and distinctive visual form. Understanding the sequence of visual perception and cognition provides designers and their clients valuable insight into what will work best. The science of perception examines how individuals recognize and interpret sensory stimuli.

Heidi Cody © 2000

Artist and cultural anthropologist Heidi Cody demonstrates how one can recognize a consumer brand just by seeing one of the letters through her artwork entitled "American Alphabet."

a. All
b. Bubblicious
c. Campbell's
d. Dawn
e. Eggo
f. Frito
g. Gatorade
h. Hebrew National
i. Icee
j. Jell-O
k. Kool-Aid
l. Lysol
m. M&M's
n. Nilla Wafers
o. Oreo
p. Pez
q. Q-tips
r. Reese's
s. Starburst
t. Tide
u. Uncle Ben's
v. V-8
w. Wisk
x. Xtra
y. York
z. Zest

The sequence of cognition

The brain acknowledges and remembers shapes first. Visual images can be remembered and recognized directly, while words have to be decoded into meaning. Reading is not necessary to be able to identify shapes, but identifying shapes is necessary to be able to read. Since a distinctive shape makes a faster imprint on memory, the importance of designing a distinctive shape is imperative in identity design.

Color is second in the sequence. Color can trigger an emotion and evoke a brand association. Distinctive colors need to be chosen carefully, not only to build brand awareness but to express differentiation. Companies such as Kodak and Tiffany have trademarked their core brand colors.

Content is third in the sequence behind shape and color. This means that the brain takes more time to process language.

Think about how IBM triggers an immediate response with its horizontal blue banded television ads. Before the ad even runs, you know it's them, and you know it's going to be intelligent and engaging.

Marjorie Gorman, SVP, Tierney Communications.

On an average day, from the moment we wake up to the time we go to sleep, we experience some three thousand marketing messages—from the medicine cabinet to the refrigerator; from the mailbox brimming with magazines, catalogues, credit card offers, and bills to the computer desktop and television; from cell phones and PDAs to the clothes we wear. In every one, a designer has considered how we, the consumer, will take in the identity of the manufacturer and remember the product.

Every company needs to differentiate itself from its competitors and gain greater market share. From an Internet café in the Scottish Highlands to a global information broker in cyberspace to a museum in Manhattan that specializes in outsider art, each has a compelling need to be distinctive. Survival of the fittest requires a brand strategy and a medium to express it. Brand identity is a critical strategy for accelerating success.

The following scenarios demonstrate when brand identity experts are needed.

New company, new product

I'm starting a new business. I need a business card and a website.

We've developed a new product, and it needs a name and a logo yesterday.

We need to raise millions of dollars. The campaign needs to have its own identity.

We're going public in the fall. We need to launch a world-class brand.

We need to raise venture capital, even though we don't have our first customer.

Name change

Our name no longer fits who we are and the businesses we're in.

We need to change our name because of a trademark conflict, and then we need to revise all of our materials.

Our name has negative connotations in the new markets we're serving.

Our name misleads customers.

Businesses have an evolving need for brand identity. Think of the entrepreneurs who started out in a garage or basement and have grown their firms into successful publicly owned companies. For a designer creating brand identity, it's important to listen to the dreams of even the smallest entrepreneurs. Think about their need to communicate: first with their earliest customers and, as they create success, with their distributors and vendors, and on through the growth cycle to the venture capital firm and shareholders.

Revitalize a brand	**Revitalize a brand identity**	**Create an integrated system**	**When companies merge**

Revitalize a brand

We want to reposition and renew the corporate brand.

We're no longer in the business that we were in when we founded our company.

We need to communicate more clearly about who we are.

We're going global—we need a brand identity that helps us enter new world markets.

No one knows who we are.

Our stock is devalued.

We want to appeal to a new and more affluent market.

Revitalize a brand identity

We are a great company with cutting-edge products. We look behind the times.

Will our identity work on the web?

Our identity doesn't position us shoulder to shoulder with our competitors.

We have eighty divisions and an inconsistent nomenclature program. We're all over the place.

I'm embarrassed when I give out our business card. We're a big business, and the card sends the wrong signal.

Everyone in the world recognizes our icon, but let's face it—she needs a face-lift. She needs to look like she lives in the twenty-first century.

We love our symbol—it is known by our market. The problem is you can't read our logotype.

Create an integrated system

We don't present a consistent face to our customers.

We have a lack of visual consistency, and we need a new brand architecture to deal with acquisitions.

Our packaging is not distinctive. Our competitors look better than us, and their sales are going up.

All of our product literature looks like it comes from different companies.

We need to look strong and communicate that we are one global company.

Every division does their own thing when marketing. It's inefficient, frustrating, and not cost-effective. Everyone is reinventing the wheel.

When companies merge

We want to send a clear message to our stakeholders that this is a merger of equals.

We want to communicate that 1 + 1 = 4.

We want to build on the brand equity of the merging companies.

We need to send a strong signal to the world that we are the new industry leader.

We need a new name.

How do we evaluate our acquisition's brand and fold it into our brand architecture?

Branding is big business. The sheer breadth of consulting firms that "do branding" is multiplying each day. From global brand and design consultancies and interactive specialists to individual experts in design, marketing, and public relations, the choice for any client may be daunting. In the old days, the differences between a branding consultancy, a design firm, and an advertising agency were obvious. As in many other arenas, convergence has come to branding. Virtual teams abound. And everyone wants the business.

There are no absolute criteria for what type of firm is the right fit for a company. An agency qualified to deliver a vast media campaign may not necessarily have the core competencies to create a brand identity. Developing a world-class brandmark, an integrated identity system, and a sustainable brand architecture is a rigorous design discipline that requires experience.

Some companies need a firm that can deliver all the components—that is, global brand strategy to brand asset management. Some companies have a strategy in place and need a world-class designer to reposition the brand. Other companies need a firm that knows how to create a look and feel, and translate that into an integrated system that works across divisions or products or cultures. And still others may need specialists, such as package and environmental designers, communication architects, or naming experts.

The process is the process, but then you need a spark of genius.

Brian P. Tierney, Esq., founder/chairman, Tierney Communications

Brand identity is a unique and sustainable symbol that synthesizes big ideas. It works across media to build awareness and loyalty and spearheads an integrated program.

Beginning at top left:

Cingular Wireless:
VSA Partners

BP:
Landor Associates

Presbyterian Church:
Malcolm Grear Designers

The Franklin Institute Science Museum:
Allemann, Almquist & Jones

Zoom:
WGBH Boston

Citi:
Pentagram

Apple Computer:
Rob Janov

Sanctum:
Frankfurt Balkind

Center City District::
Joel Katz Design Associates

Mobil:
Chermayeff & Geismar

JoongAng Ilbo:
Infinite

Pharmacia:
Landor Associates

NBC:
Chermayeff & Geismar

TimeWarner:
Chermayeff & Geismar

92:
Louise Fili

Tusk:
Milton Glaser

Bank of America:
Enterprise IG

Brinker Capital:
Rev Group

Foodsource:
Bonita Albertson

Sungshim Hospital:
Infinite

White House Conference for Children:
Chermayeff & Geismar

Mobil

PHARMACIA

foodsource

C 1

*Brand identity is flexible to
encourage creative thinking and
execution.*

Nickelodeon,
Viacom International:
Adams Morioka Design

*Brand identity is packaging that
beckons to be experienced.*

Tazo:
Sandstrom Design

Martha Stewart Living Omnimedia:
MSLO,
Doyle Partners

Brand identity engages the senses
and understands its customers.

Brand identity creates a unified
persona from a merger of equals.

Cingular:
VSA Partners

C 3

BP:
Landor Associates

*Brand identity communicates a
unique vision for the future.*

*Brand identity expresses the
value-added of a merger.*

Citi:
Pentagram

citi
citicredit
eciti
citif/i
citigold
citiselect
citifuture
citiphone

Brooklyn Academy of Music:
Pentagram

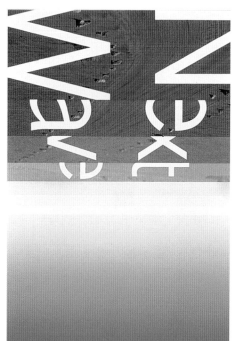

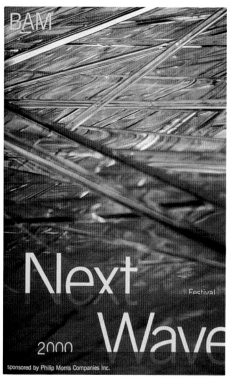

BAM 2001 Next Wave Festival
Sponsored by the Philip Morris Companies Inc.

Next
Wave
2000
Festival
Sponsored by Philip Morris Companies Inc.

*Brand identity attracts an audience
and creates a desired perception.*

*Brand identity is strategic, and
supports brand architecture across
a global spectrum of services.*

Corporation

Express

Ground

Freight

Custom Critical

Trade Networks

FedEx:
Landor Associates

C 5

*Brand identity is an integrated
program that is cohesive and
facilitates communication.*

Empire Blue Cross & Blue Shield:
Bernhardt Fudyma Design Group

*Brand identity works across languages
and cultures to build a powerful brand.*

Daehan Investment Trust Securites:
Infinite

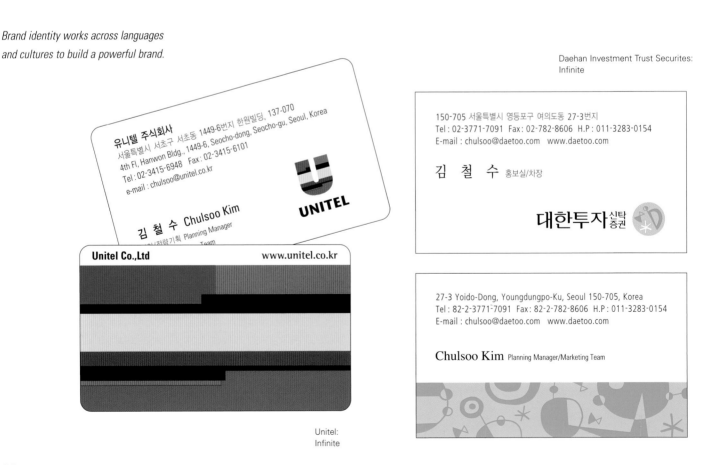

Unitel:
Infinite

*Brand identity is product and retail
design that seizes every
opportunity to delight customers.*

*Brand identity understands interactive
media and how to inspire and inform.*

Apple Computer:
Apple Industrial Design Group

Zoom:
WGBH Boston

*Brand identity builds on customer
passion and helps the sales
infrastructure sell.*

Riders Edge,
Harley Davidson:
VSA Partners

Brand identity is an ominpresent point of view that is dynamic and futuristic.

MODERN

St IVES

BRITAIN

LIVERPOOL

Tate:
Wolff Olins

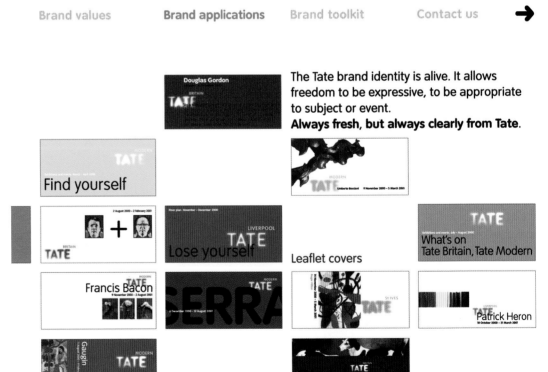

The Tate brand identity is alive. It allows freedom to be expressive, to be appropriate to subject or event.
Always fresh, but always clearly from Tate.

Find yourself

Lose yourself

Leaflet covers

What's on
Tate Britain, Tate Modern

Francis Bacon

Patrick Heron

Gaugin

Frequently a client does not know whom to call or where to start. Companies will call a wide range of firms to educate themselves and identify the right fit. Companies should hire firms with demonstrated experience and strategic imagination. Unlike advertising, which launches a new campaign each year, brand identity needs to endure. Brands, which are created and built over time, represent a major investment.

When Paul Rand designed IBM's brand identity, he was a sole practitioner. Today success depends on bringing a team, often with global experience, to the table. Some of the best brand consultancies in the world are built on design as a competitive advantage. More and more virtual teams are being created that build on "best-in-the-world" talent. Pentagram partners Michael Bierut and Paula Scher worked as a team with Michael Wolff, a preeminent global branding strategist, on the Citicorp and Travelers' merger. Lippincott & Margulies is responsible for Citibank's global signage, while Fallon Worldwide is the advertising agency.

Clients often want to work with firms with experience in their industry sector. Is this necessary? Although it may help build confidence, it is not a requirement. Unconventional thinking is often the best way to build a distinctive brand.

Extraordinary work is done for extraordinary clients.
Milton Glaser, designer

A company hires you to be a guide through an unfamiliar process. You don't know their business, and they are unfamiliar with design. The more familiar you become with their business, the more they trust your design.

Michael Bierut, Pentagram

The best identity programs embody and advance the company's brand by supporting the desired perceptions. The identity encompasses every tangible expression of the brand and becomes intrinsic to a company's culture—a constant reminder of its core values and its heritage. The mark is at the pinnacle of a branding pyramid; when the customer sees it, recognition fuels comfort and loyalty and sets the stage for a sale. A stellar identity demonstrates rather than declares a unique point of view, from the interface of a website to the design of a product to the clarity of a PowerPoint presentation. Design does make a difference.

Measuring the success of one brand over another happens every day. Business magazines regularly feature articles such as "America's Ten Best Brands," citing market share and other economic indicators. Practically every book on brand strategy will remind you of the present value of the Coca-Cola brand, which seems to increase even when the economy falters. It is more challenging, however, to measure the impact and value of brand identity. If the Coke brand is worth $83.8 billion, one needs to assume that the Coca-Cola logotype and its packaging design are brand assets that have intrinsic value.

Perception ▶ **Behavior** ▶ **Perfomance**

In Brand Leadership, by David A. Aaker and Erich Joachimsthaler, the authors build a case that "when a high level of perceived quality has been (or can be) created, raising the price not only provides margin dollars but also aids perceptions." Their basic premise is that "strong brands command a price premium." A cup of Starbucks coffee is a case in point.

Aaker has also done research suggesting that "firms experiencing the largest gains in brand equity saw their stock return average 30%; conversely, those firms with the largest losses in brand equity saw stock return average a negative 10%."

Compelling reasons to invest in brand identity
Make it easy for the customer to buy

The customer could be anyone from a person buying software on the Internet to a family buying its first home in the suburbs, from a business manager responsible for hiring a new accounting firm to an urban developer looking for an architect. Compelling brand identity presents any company, any size, anywhere with an immediately recognizable, distinctive, professional image that positions it for success. An identity helps manage the perception of a company and differentiates it from its competitors. A smart system conveys respect for the customer and makes it easy to understand features and benefits. A new product design or a better environment can delight a customer and create loyalty. An effective identity encompasses elements such as a name that is easy to remember or a package design that wants to be owned.

Make it easy for the sales force to sell

Whether it's the CEO of a global conglomerate communicating a new vision to the board, a first-time entrepreneur pitching to venture capital firms, or a financial advisor creating a need for investment products, everyone is selling. Not-for-profit organizations, whether fund-raising or soliciting new volunteers, are constantly selling as well. Strategic brand identity works across diverse audiences and cultures to build an awareness and understanding of a company and its strengths. By making intelligence visible, effective identity seeks to clearly communicate a company's unique value proposition. The coherence of communications across various media— from an advertising campaign to a business card to a sales presentation— sends a strong signal to the customer about the laserlike focus of a company.

Make it easy to build brand equity

The goal of all public companies is to increase shareholder value. A brand, or a company's reputation, is considered to be one of the most valuable company assets. Small companies and not-for-profit organizations also need to build brand equity. Their future success is dependent on building public awareness, preserving their reputations, and upholding their value. A strong brand identity will help build brand equity through increased recognition, awareness and customer loyalty, which in turn helps make a company more successful. Managers who seize every opportunity to communicate their company's brand value and what the brand stands for sleep better at night. They are building brand equity.

Regardless of the size of a company or the nature of a business, there are certain ideals that characterize the best brand identities. They hold true whether the brand identity project is about launching an entrepreneurial venture, creating a new product or service, repositioning a brand, working on a merger, or creating a retail presence. In every case, these ideals are essential to a responsible creative process. It is essential for a company to understand the larger aspirations of a brand identity.

A fairly common list of criteria for brand identity looks something like this.

An effective brand identity will:

Be bold, memorable, and appropriate

Be immediately recognizable

Provide a clear and consistent image of the company

Communicate the company's persona

Be legally protectable

Have enduring value

Work well across media and scale

Work both in black and white and in color

But these criteria do not get to the heart of brand identity. There are 1,063,164 trademarks registered with the U.S. Patent and Trademark Office. The basic question is what makes one better than another and why. What are the essential characteristics of the best identities, and furthermore, how does one define the best identities? These characteristics, or ideals, are not about a certain aesthetic. Design excellence is a given. The best identities are the most effective when they help advance the company's brand.

Ideals

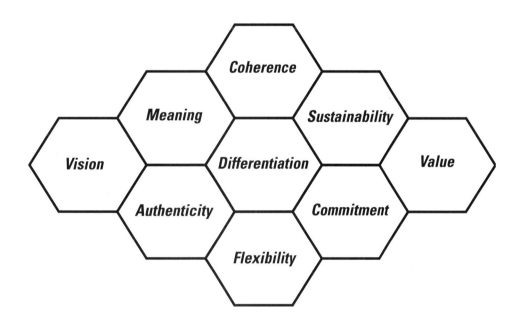

A compelling vision by an effective, articulate, and passionate leader is the foundation and the inspiration for the best brands. New ideas, enterprises, products, and services are created by individuals who have the ability to imagine what others can't see, and the tenacity to deliver what they believe is possible. Behind every new initiative is usually a dynamic individual who has the intelligence, foresight, and imagination to perceive the future in a new way and to inspire others. A vision may be expressed by a first-time entrepreneur, a museum director, or a scientist breaking new ground—it is not the exclusive province of the CEO of a global company.

The challenge to the designer is to translate that vision into a tangible expression and a visual language that resonates with all stakeholders. By necessity, the designer becomes immersed in the reality of the company—its markets, its strengths and weaknesses, its value proposition. But at some point the designer needs to focus on imagining what the future might look like. Great designers demonstrate an uncanny ability to visualize and, in effect, play back what the CEO is envisioning in her wildest dreams of the future.

The best way to predict the future is to create it.

Alan Kay, computer scientist

Listening to the CEO's vision for the newly merged company inspired our vision for the mark.

Steff Geissbuhler, partner, Chermayeff & Geismar

Time Warner:
Chermayeff & Geismar

Vision requires leadership

The best identities emerge from organizations with effective leaders, who make it a priority to articulate their vision clearly and to make it accessible. These leaders take the time to map out a strategy for the future and to motivate the people around them, whether they are customers or employees.

Brand identity needs to be a top-down initiative

Effective leaders invariably understand how to leverage symbols, prioritizing communication about the meaning of their brand. Not surprisingly, the brand identity projects that are successful are top-down initiatives, which means that a CEO has endorsed the project. This endorsement is critical because it sends a strong message to everyone involved that the project is a priority that will affect future success. Brand identity projects that do not have CEO endorsement tend to fail.

Designers need access to the vision

Designers must have access to senior leadership and to the key strategic issues. Brand identity cannot be created in a vacuum. The best identities result from designers who engage in an open dialogue with leadership. Respect must go both ways. Brand consultants are viewed as peers and team members. Designers who are denied access to senior leadership can't do their work responsibly.

Design anticipates and visualizes the future

The designer's goal is to create an identity that positions a company for growth, change, and success. That identity needs to be future-oriented and anticipate what is not yet envisioned. The designers bring their own vision to developing an identity for something that may not yet exist. From a new name through a new visual identity system, the designer's job is to bring tangible form to a vision for the future.

Great leaders see the future, set a course, and pursue it relentlessly. They conquer the present despite criticism, ambiguity, adversity. They reflect on, learn from, and weave patterns from the past. Great leaders possess the humility, optimism, passion, and wisdom to inspire others and evoke their full commitment.

Dr. Karol Wasylyshyn, president, Leadership Development Forum

The best brands stand for something—a big idea, a strategic position, a defined set of values, a voice that stands apart. Meaning inspires the creative process because it is an idea that is conveyed through a symbol, a word, or an action. It's the DNA of brand identity, where form is imbued with rationale and assigned deeper meaning. Understanding what a mark represents accelerates recognition. A mark with relevant and aspirational meaning fosters employee pride.

Symbols engage intelligence, imagination, emotion, in a way that no other learning does.

Georgetown University Identity Standards Manual

Nike was the goddess of victory. The logo, an abstraction of a wing, designed by Carolyn Davidson, was an appropriate and meaningful symbol for a company that marketed running shoes. The "just do it" campaign communicated such a strong point of view to the target market that the meaning of the symbol evolved into a battle cry and way of life for an entire generation.

The Mercedes-Benz brandmark was originally designed to represent vehicles on land, at sea, and in the air. In 1909, the mark was registered as a three-point star, and six years later it was set in a circle. The mark has come to be synonymous with luxury, high performance, and excellence.

Cingular's brandmark, nicknamed "Jack," stands for the pinnacle of individuality and freedom of human expression. It purports to help wireless users "make their mark" and adds a touch of humanity to an industry characterized by technological innovations and rate wars. "Jack" reminds us that our wireless needs come from our desire to communicate and express ourselves.

Meaning is distilled

Meaning comes from insight into the essence of an organization—who it is and what it wants to become. This insight results from purposeful investigation and focus. The designer's challenge is to absorb and understand an enormous amount of information and then to distill it into its purest and simplest form—a meaningful idea.

Meaning is assigned

Grasping the meaning of a brandmark is rarely immediate. Meaning needs to be explained, communicated, and nurtured. The American flag didn't become an immediately recognizable and universal symbol of freedom and democracy until it was communicated over and over again. Designers need to articulate the big idea behind a mark. Then the company needs to seize every opportunity to share the larger meaning as a way of building the culture and the brand.

Meaning builds consensus

Meaning is like a campfire. It unifies decision makers around important concepts. Meaning is a unifying strategy that enables decision makers to agree. Meaning is a rallying point that is used to build consensus with a group of decision makers. Agreement on the meaning of an identity and the essence of a brand builds critical synergy and precedes any presentation of visual solutions. Once a new identity is launched, it becomes integrated into the corporate culture and can be a visible reminder to the employees of its symbolic value.

Meaning evolves over time

As companies grow, the nature of their businesses may change significantly. Similarly, the meaning assigned to a brandmark may evolve from its original core idea. Meaning becomes amplified over time as the company and its culture become stronger. Meaning may also be redefined by customer perceptions and may add a new dimension to what the brand stands for based on their personal point of view and experience.

Mitsubishi Corporation's three-diamond mark stands for quality and reliability and embodies a 130-year-old commitment to earning the trust and confidence of people worldwide. Protecting the integrity of the mark is a top priority. Designed by Yataro Iwasaki, each diamond represents a core principle: corporate responsibility to society, integrity and fairness, and international understanding through trade.

The CBS eye has been the television's network symbol for over a half century. It has remained unchanged, and has retained its original powerful, all seeing iconic quality. Originally inspired by the human eye paintings on the side of Shaker barns to ward off evil, it is a highly recognized symbol around the world. Designed by William Golden, it was one of the first symbols designed to function primarily on the screen.

19

The brand identity must be an authentic expression of an organization—its unique vision, goals, values, voice, and personality. The design and messages emerge from who it is, and anticipate what it will become. The design must be appropriate to the company, its target market, and the business sector in which it operates.

In psychology, authenticity refers to self-knowledge and to making decisions and choices that are congruent with that self-knowledge. Similarly, an organization's brand and identity needs to be aligned with its heritage and its vision. Authentic identities emerge from a process that is both investigative and intuitive.

Authenticity is not possible without an organization having clarity about its market, positioning, value proposition, and competitive difference.

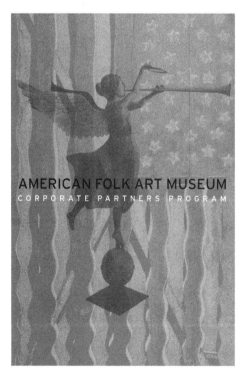

The American Folk Art Museum's identity program designed by Pentagram honors both constituencies within folk art: the traditionalists and "outsider" artists, who are self-taught and contemporary. Patterns and pieced techniques that characterize folk art are used in the logotype design and a multitude of applications from banners and brochures to mugs and shopping bags. Objects from the collection have become elements of the identity and appear in a range of eclectic treatments from silhouettes to mezzotints. The identity also reflects the architecture of the new museum building by Tod Williams Billie Tsien & Associates, which has a facade of cast-metal panels. The environmental graphics were also designed to harmonize with the new building and to reveal a "sense of the hand."

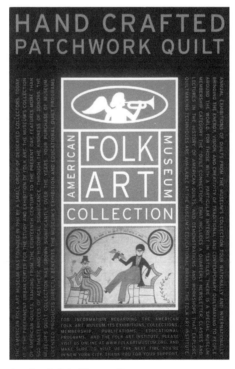

American Folk Art Museum: Pentagram

An identity needs to embrace an organization's history but incorporate enough flexibility to evolve as that organization anticipates the future.

Woody Pirtle, partner, Pentagram

We live at a time when we are bombarded by brands. They reveal themselves in every aspect of our personal and professional spaces. Their uniqueness and differentiation determine their success. Brands always compete with each other within their business category, and at some level compete with all brands that want our attention, our loyalty, and our money. When a designer creates a brandmark, her responsibility is to create a unique symbol that is differentiated, has the power to communicate within a split second, and in many cases is smaller than a dime.

Broadcast

ABC
BBC
CBS
NBC
CNN
Fox
MTV
PBS

Airline

AeroMexico
Air Canada
KLM Royal Dutch Airlines
Quantas Airways
United Airlines
US Air
Virgin Atlantic
Northwest Airlines

Automobile

BMW
Chrysler
Ford Motor Company
Honda
Infiniti
Kia
Nissan
Volkswagen

Pharmaceutical

Eli Lilly and Company
Merck
Schering-Plough
Squibb
Wellcome
Wyeth Ayerst
Astra Zeneca
Bristol-Myers Squibb

In the twenty-first century, the only constant is ongoing change. Our institutions, technology, science, style, and vocabulary are in continuous flux, and the rate of change is accelerating. And yet designers, who are the arbiters of style, need to design identities that have sustainability. Sustainability is the inherent ability of an identity to have longevity in an environment that is in flux, characterized by future permutations that no one can predict.

Brands are messengers of trust. Credibility is communicated in part by a trademark that does not fluctuate with the economy or changing business trends. Consumers depend on trademarks to be constant, so that whenever they see them—on the crest of a building, on an ad in a magazine, or even on a baseball cap—they immediately recognize them.

Sustainability also refers to an identity's ability to transition through changing media and modes of communication. When Saul Bass designed the AT&T globe in 1984, the ability of a symbol to spin and morph through space was not a technological possibility. However, during the 2000 Olympic Games, the AT&T globe became an acrobat spinning through space in an advertising campaign that captivated viewers around the world.

Trademarks, by definition, must last well beyond the fashion of the moment.
Chermayeff & Geismar

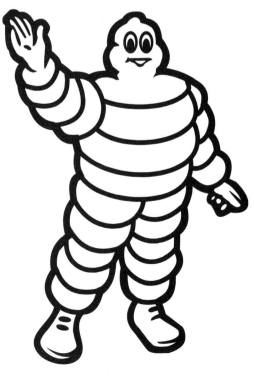

Three years after the car was born (1895), Bibendum, the name of the Michelin Man, became the company's unique symbol. Redrawn numerous times, the "tire man" is immediately recognizable around the world.

First design

Löwenbräu	1383	London Underground	1933	Westinghouse	1967
Guinness	1862	Volkswagen	1938	Metropolitan Life	1967
Olympics	1865	IKEA	1943	L'Eggs	1971
Mitsubishi	1870	CBS	1951	Eastman Kodak	1971
Nestlé	1875	NBC	1956	Nike	1971
Bass	1875	Chase Manhattan	1960	Quaker Oats	1972
John Deere	1876	IBM	1960	Atari	1973
Johnson & Johnson	1886	International Paper	1960	Merrill Lynch	1973
Coca-Cola	1887	Motorola	1960	United Way	1974
General Electric	1892	UPS	1961	Dunkin Donuts	1974
Prudential	1896	Weyerhaeuser	1961	I Love NY	1975
Michelin	1898	McDonald's	1962	Citicorp	1976
Shell	1900	General Foods	1962	PBS	1976
Nabisco	1900	Wool Bureau	1964	United	1976
Ford	1903	Rohm & Haas	1964	Apple	1977
Rolls-Royce	1905	Mobil	1965	Transamerica	1979
Mercedes-Benz	1911	Diners Club	1966	Texaco	1981
Greyhound	1926	Exxon	1966	AT&T	1984

The above dates represent the original design of the core idea. Earlier marks have been redesigned and simplified, in some cases numerous times. For example, John Deere's mark has been redesigned eight times since 1876.

The Chase trademark, designed by Chermayeff & Geismar in 1960 for the Chase Manhattan Bank, has survived sweeping change in the financial services industry, including the Chemical Bank merger in 1996 and the J.P. Morgan merger in 2000.

Whenever a customer experiences a brand, whether by using a product, talking to a service representative, or making a purchase on a website, it must feel familiar and have the desired effect. Coherence is the quality that implies that all the pieces hold together in a way that feels seamless to the customer.

An effective identity consistently applied over time is one of the most powerful marketing tools that a company can deploy. Consistency does not need to be rigid and limiting—rather, it's a baseline that is designed to build brand equity through repetition, persistence, and frequency. It's made possible by a commitment to clear brand identity standards, and is helped by a culture that values the brand and its expressions.

The goal in creating a brand identity is not just surface consistency but inner coherence.

Aubrey Balkind, CEO, Frankfurt Balkind

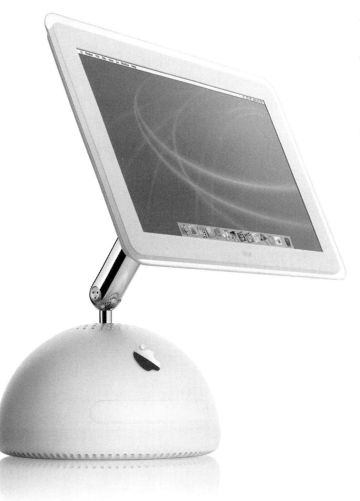

Business Week named the Apple iMac "design of the decade" in 2002, because "Good product design in and of itself can have a strong business impact. But good design that is integrated with packaging, advertising, and marketing has the greatest effect on the bottom line."

How is coherence achieved?

The brand experience feels the same, whether the customer is online, in his car, at her desk, or watching TV. This is a result of understanding the needs and preferences of the target customer and designing a brand experience that manages a desired perception. Every touchpoint is considered a brand experience.

Visual point of view

A brand identity system is unified visually and structurally. It builds on cohesive brand architecture and utilizes specially designed colors, typeface families, and formats. The identity system advances immediate recognition of the company and supports brand attributes across various media. The core identity signatures and their variations are never altered.

Messages and a unified voice

The company is clear about how it wants to be perceived, and every communication supports that goal. Consistent messages appear in sales presentations, advertising campaigns, speeches, and a myriad of other strategic marketing tools. The messages are aligned with the positioning strategy, and the tone is consistent as well.

One company strategy

The company looks the same around the world. As companies become more complex and have numerous business lines around the world selling different products, a unified global image reinforces the message that "we are one company." As companies diversify into new areas of business, consistency jumpstarts acceptance and awareness of new initiatives.

Quality

A high and uniform level of quality in visual communication imparts to the customer that the same degree of care and control is given to each of the company's products and services. This is a sustainable advantage. The company identity is a critical asset. Anything less than superior quality reduces the value of the asset on both a conscious and unconscious level.

Nomenclature

Naming that is logical and consistent within the brand architecture makes it easier for the customer to buy products and services. Communicative names are established when legal names are too cumbersome for marketing purposes. The breadth of products and services that are communicated in the clearest language improve a customer's understanding of his choices.

Building our brand requires a consistent and coordinated presentation of our identity across all communications.

ARAMARK guidelines

An identity system must continuously demonstrate an inherent flexibility. Stellar programs easily adapt to a broad range of marketing and communications applications over time to achieve sustainability. Flexibility ensures that communications stay fresh and relevant.

Designers examine how flexibility can be achieved within the brand architecture. Will the new identity facilitate brand extensions in the future? Does it have long legs? No one can say with absolute certainty what new products and services a company may offer in five or ten years. The designer, however, needs to anticipate and create a flexible infrastructure to accommodate the future.

We wanted to simplify Nickelodeon's toolkit, and focus internal creative on the core messages of the brand, with a system that was flexible and encouraged creative thinking and execution.

Sean Adams, partner,
Adams Morioka

Marketing flexibility

An effective identity positions a company for change and growth in the future. It needs to be equally effective in a range of marketing and sales tools from the website to direct mail to a news release to sales promotions and products. It supports an evolving marketing strategy.

Brand architecture flexibility

A flexible identity system doesn't lock a company into the present list of products and services. It has long legs, which means that the marketing of new businesses, products, and initiatives is facilitated by a durable and flexible system.

Standards flexibility

An effective identity system takes into consideration the multitude of professionals who will use the identity in the future, from the internal design department through the company's advertising agency. A carefully designed balance between control and creative latitude makes it easy for professionals to adhere to the identity standards while achieving specific marketing objectives.

Performance flexibility

In the design development of a logo and logotype, the designer conducts an intensive testing and design adjustment process to ensure the functionality of the signature.

An identity needs to work in:

Various scales, from smaller than a dime to as large as a billboard

Color, from full-color to two-color and one-color

Color, from Pantone through process through web-friendly

Variations of color combinations

Black and white, from a fax through a newspaper ad

Positive and negative

Electronic and print media

New media

Uniform standards

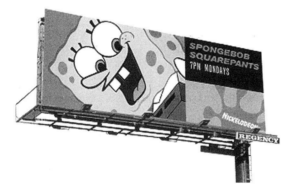

From Nick at Nite *to* Noggin, *the Nickelodeon brand grew organically and had become wildly successful, and after 15 years, disjointed. Adams Morioka's goal was to bring together Nickelodeon's world of brand extensions on the same playing field, and to unify the messages and the visual vocabulary across media. The brand needed to be more accessible and less mysterious to anyone involved with Nickelodeon.*

Nickelodeon, Viacom International:
Adams Morioka Design

A good identity does not guarantee success. It's not enough to create an effective brand name or develop a sustainable and intelligent brandmark. The best companies have a commitment to quality and to seizing every opportunity to grow their brand. An effective brand identity is tied inextricably to management's desire to nurture it. The bottom line is that identity systems need to be enforced, tweaked, monitored, and occasionally revitalized. A new brand identity program signifies the beginning of an investment of time and capital, not the end.

Perhaps the most important characteristic of a sustainable identity is taking responsibility for actively managing the asset, which includes the brand name, the trademarks, the system, and the standards. A common mistake that organizations make is the assumption that once a company has a new brand identity, the hardest work has been accomplished. In reality, the whole process is just beginning and the hard work is ahead.

Managing a brand identity system is not exclusive to large global corporations; clearly, it is easier when there is a corporate brand manager whose sole responsibility is for overseeing the brand. Small companies also need an individual who has the responsibility for overseeing the brand assets and who reports directly to the president. The mantra is to keep moving—with ongoing management, dynamic adherence to the central idea, monitoring standards that help preserve the asset, and the tools the organization needs to build its brand.

Brands, like children, need to be fed and nurtured in order to grow.

Bart Crosby, principal, Crosby Associates

Mobil graphics organization

Chermayeff & Geismar worked with Mobil for over twenty years to develop and maintain a strong identity program. This diagram, featured in the Mobil Graphic Standards, demonstrates how each of the major functions of Mobil's worldwide operations is charged with the responsibility for coordinating the Mobil identity program within each of their respective areas. All staff and field coordinators report to the corporate design manager, who reports to the chairman of the board. The organization also includes an ongoing relationship with the design and graphics consultants.

- ■ Chairman of the Board
- ☐ Corporate Design and Graphics Manager
- ■ Design Consultants
- ○ Graphic Design Advisory Group
- ● Staff Coordinators
- ● Field Coordinators

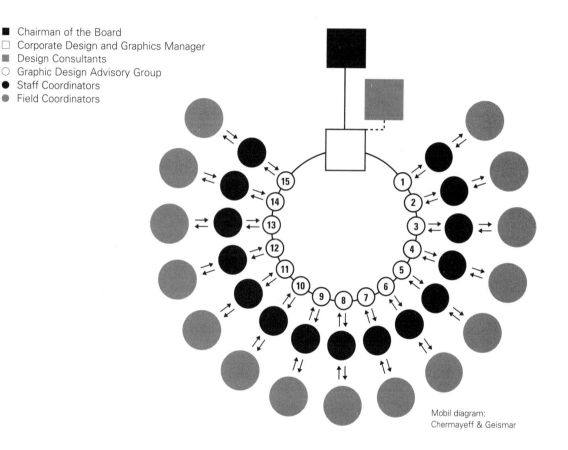

Mobil diagram:
Chermayeff & Geismar

Mobil's graphic design program is one of the primary elements of our identity program and requires the vigilance of our managers and worldwide graphics organization to insure its integrity.

Excerpt, Mobil Graphic Standards

Creating value is the indisputable goal of most organizations. The best companies consistently demonstrate their value through the superior quality of their products and services and their unswerving dedication to meeting their customer's needs. The best brand identities are the most public and widely communicated symbols of that value.

Within a company, big or small, a brand identity has value when it is viewed as an important asset by senior management. It is valued by the organization through dedication to uniform standards and the highest-quality communications. Its value is further ensured through legal protection.

Consumer brands are routinely financially valued and measured. Although a brand is more than a brandmark, the logo is virtually indistinguishable from the brand in the mind of the consumer. Effective identity is valued because it builds awareness, increases recognition, communicates uniqueness and quality, and expresses a competitive difference.

A strong brand commands a premium.

David A. Aaker and Erich Joachimsthaler, coauthors, Brand Leadership

We made the decision to adopt a new, unified identity system that would enable all of our lines of business to benefit from one another's recognition and leadership in the marketplace.

Joseph Neubauer, chairman and CEO, ARAMARK

The foundation of the CIGNA brand identity system is our trademark. It is one of CIGNA's most valuable assets and is legally protected only if it is used properly and consistently.

CIGNA Brand Identity Guidelines

We recognize the power and value created by a disciplined approach to building, protecting, and enhancing our brand. It is the hallmark by which we think, act, and behave.

Dave Reyes Guerra, Brand Management Director, Ernst & Young

Value as a symbol

As a symbol of the corporate culture, an identity engenders pride. As a symbol of the future, an identity engenders trust. It extends customer loyalty through familiarity and can build synergies across business lines.

Valued as an asset

The brand identity is viewed as a strategic business tool that actively builds trust and promotes awareness. It is viewed as a competitive advantage that has measurable results.

Commitment to value is ongoing

Adherence to the brand identity standards and the relentless pursuit of the quality of communications is an organizational priority throughout the organization.

Value is preserved through legal protection

The identity is trademarked, registered, owned, and defended. It can be protected in the range of markets that are served, whether they are local or global. The best identity standards educate employees and vendors about compliance.

Identity adds value to marketing and communications

Through consistent, smart, and clear messages, value is reinforced by strategic brand identity.

Good design is good business.

Tom Watson, chairman, IBM

A distinguishable brand adds significant value to a company's reputation and its ability to compete for clients and corporate talent. Brand identity is the essence of what your company stands for in the marketplace and with employees, as well.

Sally Hudson,
Director of Marketing,
Brinker Capital

Logos act as flags for employees and supply chain partners to rally around. And in a merger or a takeover situation, the unveiling of the new logo can be used to represent a psychological break from the past.

Helen Keyes,
Managing Director Creative,
Enterprise IG

A cohesive branding and identity system gives the tools to our salesforce to sell harder and faster.

Robert Butera, CEO,
Pennsylvania Convention Center

Brand strategy is like the corpus callosum. It connects left brain with right brain and makes the brand work. Effective brand strategy provides a central unifying idea around which all behavior, actions, and communications are aligned. It works across products and services, and is effective over time. The best brand strategies are so differentiated and powerful that they deflect the competition. They are an authentic extension of a company's persona. They are easy to talk about, whether you are the CEO or an employee.

Brand strategy builds on a vision, is aligned with business strategy, emerges from a company's history and culture, reflects an in-depth understanding of the customer's needs and perceptions. The brand strategy defines positioning, differentiation, the competitive advantage, and a unique value proposition.

Brand strategy needs to resonate with all stakeholders—external customers, the media, and internal customers (including employees, the board, and core suppliers). Brand strategy is a road map that guides marketing, makes it easier for the sales force to sell more, and provides clarity, context, and inspiration to employees.

IKEA offers good design and quality at a low price. IKEA's strategy resonates across cultures in 29 countries. Their values and company soul are aligned with their origin in a small village in Sweden where they were founded in 1943. Low prices are maintained by asking the customer to work as a partner to assemble the furniture. IKEA's mission is to "make it easy and affordable for people to live better and attain the home of their dreams." Their positioning is unböring.

Who develops brand strategy? It is usually a team of people; no one does it alone. It is a result of an extended dialogue among CEO, marketing, sales, advertising, public relations, operations, and distribution. Global companies frequently bring in brand strategists: independent thinkers and authorities, strategic marketing firms, and brand consultants. It often takes someone from the outside who is an experienced strategic and creative thinker to help a company articulate what is already there. Companies also use marketing research to determine and test the best strategies.

Sometimes a brand strategy is born at the inception of a company by a visionary, such as Anita Roddick, Steve Jobs, Martha Stewart, or Jeff Bezos. Sometimes it takes a visionary leader, such as Lou Gerstner, former CEO, IBM, to bring brand strategy to a new level because the company has become a behemoth. Companies frequently survive and prosper because they have a clear brand strategy. Companies falter because they don't have one.

The role of the consultant in developing brand strategy is to facilitate the process: asking the right questions, providing relevant input and ideas, getting key issues to surface, and achieving resolution.

Erich Sippel, president,
Erich Sippel & Company

Every senior leader in an organization must be focused and accountable for translating the brand strategy.

Betty Nelson, group director
global communications,
IMS Health.

Branding imperatives

Acknowledge that we live in a branded world.

Seize every opportunity to position your company in your customer's mind.

Communicate a strong brand idea over and over again.

Go beyond declaring a competitive advantage. Demonstrate it!

Understand the customers. Build on their perceptions, preferences, dreams, values, and lifestyles.

Identify touchpoints—places in which a customer interfaces with the product or service.

Use brand identity to create sensory magnets to attract and retain customers.

After Septemeber 11th, human values, not commercial values, have become the brand's currency of commerce...and thus, will change the way the consumer experiences a brand. The ability of brand storytellers to convey this to their consumers will give them a profound advantage over others.

Jack Cassidy, CEO,
RJHGlobal Public Relations,
London

Supporting every effective brand is a positioning strategy that drives planning, marketing, and sales. Positioning evolves to create openings in a market that is constantly changing, a market where consumers are saturated with products and messages. Positioning takes advantage of changes in demographics, technology, marketing cycles, consumer trends, and gaps in the market to find new ways of appealing to the public. Positioning allows companies to turn obstacles into opportunities.

Distinguishing a product or service becomes more and more challenging. Developed by Al Reis and Jack Trout in 1981, positioning becomes the scaffolding on which companies build their brands, strategize their planning, and extend their relationships with customers. Positioning takes into account the mix of price, product, promotion, and place (distribution), which are the four dimensions that affect sales.

Reis and Trout were convinced that each company must determine its position in the customer's mind, considering the needs of the customer, the strengths and weaknesses of that company, and the world of competition. This concept continues to be a fundamental precept in all marketing communications, branding, and advertising.

Positioning breaks through barriers of oversaturated markets to create new opportunites.

Lissa Reidel, communications guru

Henry Ford said customers could have any color they wanted as long as it was black. General Motors came along with five colors and stole the show.

What are positioning statements?

Positioning statements are short, pithy, powerful drivers in brand strategy. They are more than marketing slogans, since they summarize a promise to the customers. They also represent the company's vision of the future: the big dream, the ultimate goal, the long-term possibilities.

Positioning statements can be found on websites, in shareholder letters, and in marketing strategy documents. Identity programs and advertising campaigns are expressions of positioning strategy.

The difference between sales and marketing

Sales and marketing use similar approaches: publications, advertising, direct mail. But in a sales campaign, the focus is the product. A company that is market-driven focuses on the consumer. The product is defined and finite, but in the mind of the client there are infinite possibilities. Marketing penetrates into the psyche of the customer. The company that markets has its fingers on the pulse of the consumer.

Sneakers

In the fifties, everyone had one pair of white tennis sneakers. They were the most mundane necessities. Then sneakers were redesigned and repositioned in the consumer mind. They became endowed with celebrity status and transformed into a symbols of empowerment in the mid 1970s, when Nike and Reebok picked up on the increased interest in health, changed the perception, and raised the price. Sneakers have brand status and everyone needs more than one pair.

Water

Until the 1980s, tap water tasted good. If consumers thought about water at all, it was only that one should have eight glasses a day. Health trends coincided with the water supply becoming less than the dependable utility it had always been. The three-martini lunch was no longer hip, yet people still wanted something with cachet to drink. Presto: bottled water reassured people that they were drinking something healthy and ordering something trendy. It's slimming, it's nonalcoholic, it's pure, celebrities buy it. . . and it is affordable for everyone. How could it miss?

Big-box stores

Target created a new position for itself as a big-box store with products that were designed by some of the best designers in the world. Target's positioning is dramatically different from that of Wal-Mart, the biggest store on earth. While Wal-Mart is about the lowest price, Target's positioning is created around appeal (design) as well as necessity and price. Target has built recognition of its brand to the degree that some ad campaigns feature the Target logo in audacious applications, including fabric patterns and spots on a dog, without mentioning the company name.

Positioning is identifying the real estate in a consumer's mind that the brand will and can own.

LeRoux Jooste, VP worldwide
product planning, Cephalon

Brand architecture refers to the hierarchy of brands within a single company. It is the interrelationship of the parent company, subsidiary companies, products, and services. More importantly, the brand architecture should be a mirror of the marketing strategy. Brand identity design brings consistency, visual and verbal order, thought, and intention to disparate elements to help a company grow and market more effectively.

As companies merge with others and acquire new companies and products, the branding, nomenclature, and marketing decisions become exceedingly complex. Decision makers examine marketing, cost, time, and legal implications.

The need for brand architecture is not limited to Fortune 100 companies or for-profit companies. Any company or institution that is growing needs to evaluate which brand architecture strategy will support future growth. Most large companies that sell products and services have a mixture of strategies. There are a number of different types of brand architecture that have been identified over the years by various marketing strategists. They all basically refer to the same scenarios, and there is no right or overriding term.

Strategic questions	Consider
What are the benefits of leveraging the name of the parent company?	Visible Invisible
Does the positioning of our new entity require that we distance it from the parent?	Endorsed Branded Co-branded
Will co-branding confuse the consumer?	Generic Premium
How do we brand this new acquisition?	Primary Secondary Tertiary
Do we change the name or build on existing equity even though it was owned by a competitor?	One identity Many identities
Should we ensure that the parent company is always visible in a secondary position?	Big type Little type Bold type Mice type

Monolithic brand architecture

In this scenario, there is a strong, single master brand around which everything is unified. Customers have a clear picture of this company—its persona, its ethos, and its values—and make purchasing decisions based on loyalty. The features and benefits of the product are less important than the brand promise, because the consumer trusts the brand. The visual identity and the brand name are consistent across products and services, and in global locations. In both the corporate and consumer sectors, brand extensions are built by using generic descriptions.

Examples

Starbucks

The Vanguard Group

Mobil

FedEx

Hewlett-Packard

The Body Shop

Virgin

Mercedes-Benz

Martha Stewart

Subbrand or subsidiary brand architecture

In this scenario, a branded subsidiary, product, or service is combined with the core brand identity. Either the master brand dominates or the two brands serve as co-drivers.

Examples

Suburu Outback

Sony Walkman

Adobe Acrobat

Nike Air Jordan

Endorsed brand architecture

In this scenario, there is marketing synergy between the product or division name and the parent name. The product or division has a clearly defined market presence, but it benefits from the association and visiblity of the parent. The parent, in essence, endorses the product, service, or division.

Examples

iPod and Apple Computer

Polo and Ralph Lauren

Oreo and Nabisco

PowerPoint and Microsoft

Navy Seals and the U.S. Navy

Sesame Street and PBS

Residence Inn and Marriott

Pluralistic brand architecture

In this scenario, a parent has a series of products that are well-known consumer brands. All marketing resources are focused on selling these brands to their specific target markets. The name of the parent may be either invisible or inconsequential to the consumer. Many parent companies develop a system for corporate endorsement that is tertiary. The parent name is primarily recognized by the investment community.

Examples

Wharton (University of Pennsylvania)

Tang (Philip Morris Companies)

Godiva Chocolates (Campbell Soup)

Jeep Cherokee (DaimlerChrysler)

Prozac (Lilly)

Ritz-Carlton (Marriott)

A well-chosen name for a company, product, or service is a valuable asset as well as a workhorse. Whether a company is a multinational corporation or a sole proprietorship, a name directly affects brand perception and, ultimately, its success.

A name is transmitted hundreds of thousands of times each and every day—from the text of an e-mail to answering the phone, and on every business card, marketing brochure, website, and product. A bad name can hinder marketing efforts, either through miscommunication or simply because people can't pronounce it or remember it. A bad name can also subject a company to unnecessary legal risks.

Finding a new name that is legally available is an increasingly difficult challenge. Naming requires a creative, disciplined, and strategic approach.

In today's competitive world, a name must function as a total messenger.

Naseem Javed, author, Naming for Power

Naming myths
Naming a company is easy, like naming a baby
Naming is a rigorous and exhaustive process. Frequently hundreds of names are reviewed prior to finding one that is legally available and works.

I'll know it when I hear it
People often indicate that they will be able to make a decision after hearing a name once. In fact, good names are strategies and need to be examined, tested, sold, and proven.

We'll just do the search ourselves
Intellectual property lawyers need to conduct extensive searches to ensure that there are no conflicting names and to make record of similar names. It's too large a risk—names need to last over time.

We can't afford to test the name
Various thoughtful techniques must be utilized to analyze the effectiveness of a name to ensure that its connotations are positive in the markets served.

Qualities of an effective name

Meaningful
It communicates something about the nature of the company to its target market. It supports the image that the company wants to convey.

Memorable
It is distinctive as well as easy to remember, pronounce, and spell. It is differentiated from the competition and has a unique personality.

Future-Oriented
It positions the company for growth, change, and success. It has long legs: it allows a company to build brand extensions with ease. It is modular and works on the Internet. It has sustainability.

Protectable
It can be owned and trademarked. The domain is available.

Positive
It has positive connotations in the markets served. It has no strong negative connotations.

Visual
It lends itself well to graphic presentation and multimedia.

Types of names

Founder
Many great companies have been named after the founders: Dell Computer, Chrysler, Merrill Lynch, Merck, Charles Schwab. Mercedes was the name of the granddaughter of the founder. The benefit of using a name is that it is easier to protect. It satisfies an ego. The downside is that in itself it is not very descriptive of what a company does.

Descriptive
These names accurately convey the nature of the business, such as Priceline.com, Toys R Us, or E*TRADE. The benefit of a descriptive name is that it clearly communicates the intent of the company. The potential disadvantage is that as a company grows and decides to diversify, the name may become limiting. Some descriptive names are difficult to protect since they are so generic.

Fabricated
These names are made up, such as Sageo, Exxon, Kodak, Xerox, or Agilent. The advantage of this type of name is that it may be easier to copyright. It is certainly distinctive, but a company must invest a significant amount of capital into educating its market as to the nature of the business, service or product. Häagen-Dazs is a fabricated foreign word that has been extremely effective in the consumer market.

Metaphor
Things, places, people, animals, processes, mythological names, or foreign words are used in this type of name to allude to a quality of a company. These names are interesting to visualize and often can tell a good story. Oracle, Nike, and Sprint are some excellent examples. Some names are derivative from Latin words, such as Derivium Capital and Altria.

Acronym
These names are difficult to remember, difficult to copyright, and hard to look up in the phone book. Acronyms such as IBM and GE became well known only after the companies established themselves with the full spelling of their names. There are so many acronyms that new ones are increasingly more difficult to learn and require a substantial investment in advertising. Other examples: USAA, AARP, DKNY, and CNN.

Combinations of the above
Some of the best names combine these categories. Some good examples are Cingular Wireless, Citibank, and Templeton Funds. It is well documented that customers and investors like names that they can understand.

It's hard to think of a well-known brand without thinking of its tagline. The tagline is a short phrase that captures a company's brand essence, personality, and positioning, and distinguishes it from its competitors. The taglines of many companies have become part of our popular culture. Through their frequent and consistent exposure in the media, their familiarity influences consumers' buying behavior by evoking an emotional response. Traditionally used in advertising, companies are increasingly using taglines on other marketing collateral as the centerpiece of their positioning strategy.

Taglines frequently have a shorter life span than visual identities. Like advertising campaigns, they are more susceptible to marketplace and lifestyle changes. Deceptively simple, they are not arbitrary. They grow out of an intensive creative and strategic process.

Taglines were once called slogans. The origin of the word *slogan* came from the Gaelic *slaughgaiirm,* used by Scottish clans to mean "war cry." Slogans have been an integral part of consumer advertising since the Civil War. In the latter part of the twentieth century, many slogans became shorter and punchier, and acceptable for any kind of company.

A tagline is a slogan, clarifer, mantra, company statement or guiding principle that describes, synopsizes or helps create an interest.

Debra Koontz Traverso, author, Outsmarting Goliath

Did you know

Merrill Lynch and Key Bank have eliminated their logotype from their advertising signature, and just use the tagline and the symbol.

Taglines sum up the sell, and the best of them evoke an emotional response.

Jerry Selber, LevLane

Tagline basics

1 A tagline must be short.

2 It must be differentiated from its competitors.

3 It must be unique.

4 It must capture the brand essence and positioning.

5 It must be easy to say and remember.

6 It cannot have any negative connotations.

7 It is typically displayed in a small font.

8 It can be protected and trademarked.

9 It evokes an emotional response.

10 It is difficult to create.

Types of taglines

There are a number of different types of tagline strategies and styles:

Imperative

Commands action and usually starts with a verb

Descriptive

Describes the service, product, or brand promise

Superlative

Positions the company as best in class

Provocative

Thought-provoking; frequently a question

Specific

Establishes leadership of a category

A cross-section of taglines

Company	Tagline
Imperative	
Nike	Just do it
Hewlett-Packard	Invent
Apple Computer	Think different
Toshiba	Don't copy. Lead.
Mutual of Omaha	Begin today
Conseco	Step up
Honda	Simplify
Kinko's	Express yourself
Descriptive	
PNC	The thinking behind the money
UPS	Moving at the speed of business
Concentrics	People. Process. Results.
Bank of America	Embracing ingenuity
MSNBC	The whole picture
Infiniti	Accelerating the future
Merrill Lynch	Bullish on America
Ernst & Young	From thought to finish
Allstate	You're in good hands
AT&T	Your world. Close at hand.
GE	We bring good things to life
Superlative	
BMW	The ultimate driving machine
Lufthansa	There's no better way to fly
National Guard	Americans at their best
Hoechst	The future in life sciences
DeBeers	A diamond is forever
Provocative	
Cingular Wireless	What do you have to say?
Sears	Where else?
Microsoft	Where are you going today?
Mercedes-Benz	What makes a symbol endure?
Dairy Council	Got milk?
Viagra	Let the dance begin
Philips	Let's make things better
Specific	
Cisco Systems	Empowering the Internet generation
CDW	Computing solutions built for business
PeopleSoft	People power the Internet
Volkswagen	Drivers wanted
eBay	Happy hunting
Minolta	The essentials of imaging

From literal through symbolic, from word-driven to image-driven, the world of brandmarks expands each day. Designed with an almost infinite variety of shapes and personalities, brandmarks can be assigned to a number of general categories. The boundaries between these categories are pliant, and many marks may combine elements of more than one category. Is there a compelling practical reason to categorize them? Although there are no hard-and-fast rules to determine the best type of visual identifier for a particular type of company, the designer's process is to examine a range of solutions based on both aspirational and functional criteria. The designer will determine a design approach that best serves the needs of the client, and create a rationale for each distinct approach.

Topology of Marks and Logotypes

LOGOTYPE ·······➤ WORDMARK ·······➤ MARKS INCLUDING LETTERFORMS ·······➤

◀ ·

LITERAL
WORD-DRIVEN
CONCEPTUALLY SIMPLE

TYPOGRAPHIC

CHARACTER

PICTORIAL

ABSTRACT/ SYMBOLIC

SYMBOLIC
IMAGE-DRIVEN
CONCEPTUALLY COMPLEX

NONTYPOGRAPHIC

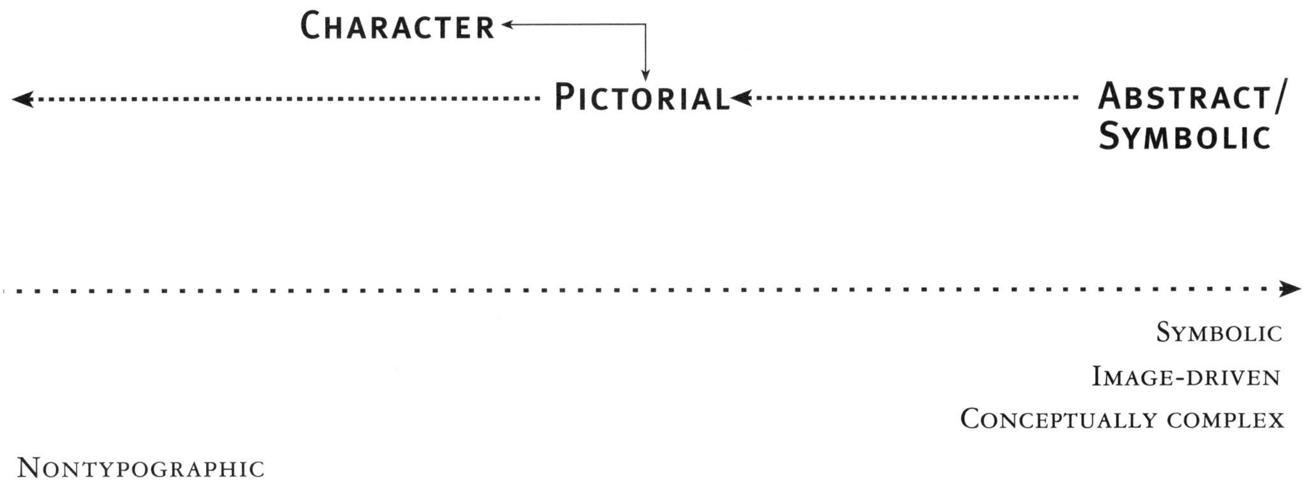

Diagram Concept by Joel Katz,
Joel Katz Design Associates

Synonyms
Brandmark
Trademark
Symbol
Mark
Logo

A wordmark is a freestanding word or words. It may be a company name or an acronym. The best wordmarks imbue a legible word(s) with distinctive font characteristics, and may integrate abstract elements or pictorial elements. The distinctive tilted *E* in Dell activates and strengthens the one-syllable name. The IBM acronym has transcended enormous technological change in its industry.

Alvin Ailey:
Chermayeff & Geismar

BRAUN

IBM

Mobil

DELL

Kubota

BEST

PONVIA

d'g't'l

Braun:
Wolfgang Schmittel redesign

IBM: Paul Rand

Children's Television Workshop:
Milton Glaser

Tazo: Sandstrom Design

Mr. and Mrs. Aubrey Hair:
Woody Pirtle

Mobil:
Chermayeff & Geismar

Dell Computer:
Siegel & Gale

Kubota: Pentagram

Best:
Chermayeff & Geismar

Ponvia Technology:
Crosby Associates

Digital Composition:
Crosby Associates

The single letter is frequently used by designers as a distinctive graphic focal point for a brandmark. The letter is always a unique and proprietary design that is infused with significant personality and meaning. The letterform acts as a mnemonic device, i.e., the *M* for Motorola, the *H* for Herman Miller. The Westinghouse mark by Paul Rand represents the ideal marriage between letterform and symbolism.

Opposite page from left to right:

Arvin Industries: Bart Crosby

Aids Project Rhode Island:
Malcolm Grear Designers

Badger Meter: Bart Crosby

Bay State Abrasives:
Malcolm Grear Designers

Champion International Corporation:
Crosby Associates

Lifespan: Malcolm Grear Designers

NEPTCO: Malcolm Grear Designers

Providence Journals:
Malcolm Grear Designers

Seatrain Lines:
Chermayeff & Geismar

Sherrill Associates:
Allemann, Almquist & Jones

Goertz Fashion House:
Allemann Almquist & Jones

Fine Line Features:
Woody Pirtle

Landa Pharmaceutical:
Pentagram

Westinghouse:
Paul Rand

Energy Department Store:
Katz Wheeler Design

JoongAng Ilbo: Infinite

Owens Illinois:
Chermayeff & Geismar

Rogers Ford, architecture firm:
Summerford Design

Lifemark Partners: Rev Group

Brokers Insurance: Rev Group

Dallas Opera: Woody Pirtle

A pictorial mark uses a literal and recognizable image. The image itself may allude to the name of the company or its mission, or it may be symbolic of a brand attribute. The eagle of the U.S. Postal Service is both a symbol of America and a symbol of speed and dependablity. A character mark is created to embody brand attributes or values, usually of a product-based brand. From the Michelin Man to Smokey the Bear to the Energizer bunny, these characters can become central to advertising campaigns, and can quickly become cultural icons.

Active Aging Association, Tokyo:
Chermayeff & Geismar

British Telecom:
Wolff Olins

This page from left to right:

CIGNA: Landor Associates

Greyhound USA: Raymond Loewy

John Deere: John Dreyfuss redesign

Lacoste: Robert George

March of Dimes:
Pentagram

Merrill Lynch: King-Casey

Flab Bat 25/ a division of the Swiss
Army: Allemann Almquist & Jones

NBC: Chermayeff & Geismar

PBS: Chermayeff & Geismar

Tusk: Milton Glaser

World Wildlife Foundation:
Landor Associates, redesign

Angels in America: Milton Glaser

Michelin Man: original concept by
Marius Rossillon

Children's Rehabiliation Hospital:
Allemann Almquist & Jones

Chicago 2001: Crosby Associates

An abstract mark uses visual form to convey a big idea or a brand attribute. These marks, by their nature, can provide strategic ambiguity, and work effectively for large companies with numerous and unrelated divisions. Marks such as Chase's have survived a series of mergers easily. Abstract marks are especially effective for service-based and technology companies; however, they are extremely difficult to design well.

Penns Landing is a mixed use riverfront development with public open space juxtaposed to commercial, retail, and residential buildings. Joel Katz's symbol design is based on the semaphore (nautical sign) for P for Penns Landing and Philadelphia, a historic city of squares. The mark is designed to communicate that Penns Landing is the square on the water.

This page from left to right:

Chase Manhattan:
Chermayeff & Geismar

United Banks of Colorado:
Chermayeff & Geismar

Torin:
Chermayeff & Geismar

Screen Gems:
Chermayeff & Geismar

Concentrics: Rev Group

Ilona Financial Group: Rev Group

Intersection: Rev Group

JDM Partners: Rev Group

The Field Museum:
Crosby Associates

Merck: Chermayeff & Geismar

Pan American World Congress of
Architects: Chermayeff & Geismar

Sacred Heart Hospital: Infinite

Advocate Health Care:
Crosby Associates

Daejon University: Infinite

Cherry Vale Development Corporation:
Crosby Associates

The brand identity process is a proven and disciplined method for creating and implementing an identity. It is a rigorous process demanding a combination of investigation, strategic thinking, design excellence, and project management skills. It requires an extraordinary amount of patience, an obsession for getting it right, and an ability to synthesize vast amounts of information.

Regardless of the nature of the client and the complexity of the engagement, the process remains the same. What changes is the depth with which each phase is conducted, the amount of time and resources allocated, and the size of the team, on both the identity firm and client sides.

The process is defined by distinct phases with logical beginning and ending points, which allow decision making at the appropriate intervals. Eliminating steps or reorganizing the process may present an appealing way to cut costs and time, but doing so can pose substantial risks and impede long-term benefits. The process, when done right, can achieve remarkable results.

Most processes leave out the stuff that no one wants to talk about: magic, intuition and leaps of faith.

Michael Bierut, partner, Pentagram

phase **1.**

RESEARCH AND ANALYSIS

Clarify vision, strategies, goals, and values

Research stakeholders' needs and perceptions

Conduct an internal, competitive, technology, and legal audit

Interview key management

Evaluate existing brands and brand architecture

phase **2.**

BRAND STRATEGY

Synthesize learnings

Clarify brand strategy

Develop a positioning platform

Co-create brand attributes

Present brand brief

Create a naming strategy

Why the process is a competitive advantage

Assures the client that a proven method is being used to achieve business results

Accelerates understanding and acceptance of the investment of necessary time and resources

Engenders trust and confidence in the identity firm

Positions project management as smart, efficient, and cost-effective

Builds credibility and strengthens identity solutions

Sets expectations for the complexity of the process

Provides a road map for managing the process

Navigating through the political process—building trust—building relationships—it's everything.

Paula Scher, partner, Pentagram

phase **3.**

DESIGN CONCEPT

Visualize the future

Design brand identity

Finalize brand architecture

Examine applicability

Present visual strategy

phase **4.**

BRAND EXPRESSIONS

Finalize identity solution

Initiate trademark protection

Prioritize and design applications

Design identity program

Apply brand architecture

phase **5.**

MANAGING ASSETS

Build synergy around new brand

Develop launch strategy and plan

Launch internally first

Launch externally

Develop standards and guidelines

Nurture brand champions

Astute project management is critical to achieving the long-term goals of a brand identity project. Responsible project management sets the foundation for mutual respect, confidence, and long-term success. The identity process demands a range of skills on both the client side and the identity firm side. It demands leadership and creativity working hand in hand with planning, coordinating, analyzing, understanding, and managing time, resources, and money. On top of organization and discipline, the process requires patience, enthusiasm, and laserlike focus on achieving the end goal.

How long will it take?

All clients have a sense of urgency, regardless of the size and nature of the company. There are no shortcuts to the process, and eliminating steps may be detrimental to achieving long-term goals. Developing an effective and sustainable identity takes time. There are no instant answers, and a commitment to a responsible process is imperative.

Time factors

The length of a brand identity project is affected by the following factors:

Size of organization

Complexity of business

Number of markets served

Type of market: global, national, regional, local

Nature of problem

Research required

Legal requirements (merger or public offering)

Decision-making process

Number of decision makers

Number of applications

Project management process

Team protocol

- Clearly define team goals
- Establish roles and responsibilities
- Understand policies and procedures
- Identify client project manager + team
- Identify firm contact + team
- Circulate pertinent contact data

Team commitment

- Open communications
- Confidentiality
- Dedication to brand
- Mutual respect

Benchmarks and schedule

- Identify deliverables
- Identify key dates
- Develop project schedule
- Update schedules as necessary
- Develop task matrix

Decision-making protocol

- Establish process
- Determine decision makers
- Clarify benefits and disadvantages
- Put all decisions in writing

Who manages the project?

Client side

For a small business, the founder or owner is invariably the project leader, the key decision maker, and the visionary. In larger companies, the project manager is whomever the CEO designates: the director of marketing and communications, the brand manager, the public relations firm on retainer, or maybe even the CFO.

The project manager must be someone with authority who can make things happen, given the enormous amount of coordination, scheduling, and information gathering. He also must have direct access to the CEO and other decision makers. In larger companies, the CEO usually forms a brand team, which may include representatives from different divisions or business lines. Although this team may not be the ultimate decision-making group, it must have access to the key decision makers.

Identity firm side

In a large brand consultancy, a dedicated project manager is the key client contact. Various tasks are handled by specialists, from market researchers and business analysts to naming specialists and designers. In small to midsize firms, the principal may be the main client contact, senior creative director, and senior designer. A firm may bring on specialists as needed, from market research firms to naming experts, to create a virtual team that is best in class.

Characteristics of the best project managers

Developed by Praxis Consulting Group.

Focus: ability to see and maintain the big picture and at the same time break it down into smaller ordered pieces; ability to keep moving despite challenges and constraints

Discipline: ability to plan, track numerous tasks, and balance time and cost factors

Strong communication skills: ability to communicate clearly, respectfully, and in a timely fashion to keep all team members fully informed

Empathy: ability to understand and respond to the needs, viewpoints, and perspectives of all players in the project

Effective management skills: ability to define needs, priorities, and tasks; make decisions; flag problems; and hold people accountable

Flexibility (adaptability): ability to stay focused and in control when things go wrong or change in midstream

Creative problem-solving ability: willingness to see problems as challenges to address rather than as obstacles

Insight: understanding of policies, procedures, corporate culture, key people, politics

Communications protocol	*Documentation*	*Information gathering*	*Legal protocol*	*Presentation protocol*
- Establish document flow - Decide who gets copied and how - Put everything in writing - Create agendas - Circulate meeting notes - Develop Internet project site if appropriate to scale of project	- Date all documents - Date each sketch process - Assign version numbers to key documents	- Determine responsibilities - Determine dates - Identify proprietary information - Develop task matrix - Develop audit	- Identify intellectual property resource - Understand compliance issues - Gather confidentiality statements	- Circulate goals in advance - Hand out agenda at meeting - Determine presentation medium - Develop uniform presentation system - Obtain approvals and sign-offs - Identify next steps

Managing decisions

Decision making can be designed to be an intelligent, engaging process that builds trust and helps organizations make the right choices to build their brand. Most people can recall a scenario where the wrong decision was made because of either politics or too many decision makers. Experts in the social sciences believe that decisions made by large groups tend to be more conservative and less visionary (inspired) than decisions made by small groups. Yet organizational development experts may tell you that decision by consensus has the potential to result in higher-quality decisions because the organization uses the resources of its members.

The path to reconciling these seemingly conflicting points of view leads to a brand champion or CEO with strong leadership skills, someone who can elicit ideas and opinions from a wider group without succumbing to group-think. In an ideal situation, the final decision makers, regardless of the size of the organization, should be kept to a very small group led by the CEO. The group makes informed choices that are aligned with the vision of the organization, and is involved throughout the process at key decision points, i.e., agreement on goals, brand strategy, names, taglines, and brandmarks.

Smart organizations often use the branding process to involve as many stakeholders as possible in the vision and mission of the organization, and to provide customer insights. Companies employ methods ranging from interviews and employee surveys through focus groups and presentations to elicit the best and most varied thinking. When it is done well, people throughout the organization feel valued and begin to "own" the new brand.

All the best strategic and creative thinking in the world can go amuck without an intelligent decision making process.

Emily Cohen, consultant to creative professionals

Essential characteristics of optimum decision making

1 CEO leads small group that includes marketing brand champions

2 Entire process is clearly communicated to key stakeholders

3 Decisions are aligned with vision and goals

4 All members are trusted and respected

5 Agreement on goals and positioning strategy precedes creative strategy

6 All relevant information and concerns are noted and tracked

7 Pros and cons are always fully discussed

8 Commitment is made to communicate about the brand through all levels of the organization

9 Focus groups are used as a tool, not as a thought leader

10 Decisions are communicated internally first

11 Confidentiality is honored

Challenging scenarios

When the CEO is not involved

When new decision makers get involved in the middle of the process

When team members' opinions are not respected

When critical steps are eliminated in the process to save money and time

When personal aesthetics get confused with functional criteria

Mergers and acquisitions

The financial stakes are high and the work is being done within a very compressed time frame. Decisions need to be made quickly and quietly in what is usually a tense atmosphere, where many other concerns are vying for the attention of the leadership. Another challenge is the difficulty of collecting input from a broad constituency when confidentiality is critical. Frequently, brand names and marks are used in a symbolic chess match by the merging leadership. It is critical to keep all team members focused on the end goal and to stay calm.

Red flags

The CEO (or global brand manager) doesn't have time to meet with you.

I'll know it when I see it.

We're going to show all the partners to see if they like it.

We're going to use focus groups to help us make the right decision.

We know that's the better design but the CEO's husband doesn't like it.

We want to show the entire list of 573 names to the CEO and let her decide what she likes best.

Let's vote on our favorites.

The best identities have business acumen as well as aesthetic value. The first priority is to understand the organization—its mission, vision, target markets, corporate culture, competitive advantage, strengths and weaknesses, marketing strategies, and challenges for the future. Learning must be focused and accelerated. Clients hire firms with the intellectual capacity to understand the business as a way of ensuring that the solutions are linked to business strategies and goals.

Understanding comes from various sources—from reading strategic documents and business plans to interviewing key stakeholders. Requesting the appropriate information from a client is the first step, prior to any interviewing of key management or stakeholders. Listening to the organization's vision and strategies for the future forms the nucleus of the creative process for a new identity. Interviewing key people face-to-face provides invaluable insight into the voice, cadence, and personality of an organization. Frequently, ideas and strategies emerge during an interview that may never have been recorded before.

Understanding also may be achieved by experiencing the organization from a customer's perspective, gaining insight from navigating the website, and seeing how easy it is to understand the product offerings, receive a sales pitch, or use the products. The goal is to uncover the essence of this company, and also to understand how that organization fits into the larger competitive environment.

Baseline information to request

Request these business background materials to learn more about the organization prior to any interviews. If it's a public company, examine what financial analysts say about the company's performance and future prospects.

Mission	*Existing marketing research*
Vision	*Cultural assessments*
Values statement	*Employee surveys*
Value proposition	*CEO speeches*
Organization chart	*Press releases*
Strategic planning documents	*News clippings*
Business plans	*History*
Marketing plans	*Domains*
Annual reports	*Intranet access*

Interviewing key stakeholders

Interviewing key management is routinely done face-to-face. Frequently, the identity firm principal will tape the interview and transcribe it, as opposed to taking notes. This facilitates more eye contact and a better-quality interview. If necessary, interviewing can be done over the telephone. Building trust is another agenda—the quality of the questions and the rapport established in the interview set the tone for an important relationship. Encourage individuals to be brief and succinct. Do not provide questions in advance, if possible, since spontaneous answers may be more insightful. It is absolutely critical to read through the baseline information about the company before any interview is conducted.

The following questions should be customized prior to interviewing. It's important to convey that you have already examined the documents provided. The list of who is interviewed is co-created with a client. It is best to keep interviews under one hour in length.

Core interview questions

1 What is your mission? What are your three most important goals?

2 Why was this company created?

3 Describe your products or services.

4 Who is your target market?

5 Prioritize your stakeholders in order of importance. How do you want to be perceived by each audience?

6 What is your competitive advantage? Why do your customers choose your product or service over others? What do you do better than anyone else?

7 Who is your competition? Is there a competitor that you admire most, and why?

8 How do you market your product and services?

9 What are the trends and changes that affect your industry?

10 Where will you be in five years? In ten years?

11 How do you measure success?

12 What values and beliefs unify your personnel and drive their performance?

13 What are the potential barriers to the success of your product or service?

14 Place yourself in the future. If your company could do anything or be anything, what would it be?

15 If you could communicate a single message about your company, what would it be?

From face to face interviews to online surveys and usability testing, market research takes many forms. Research is not a black box that automatically provides an answer. Rather, it is a tool that seeks to probe and reveal new insights. Skeptics say that research only confirms intuition. Believers hold that it is a necessary foundation for meaningful brand strategy and identity design.

Market research is the gathering and evaluation of data regarding preferences for products, services, and brands. It's a tool that is used to understand attitudes, perceptions, and behavior of potential or existing customers in various market segments. It is also used to identify and clarify segments that may provide the greatest opportunities for a company in the future.

Large brand consultancies typically have developed proprietary research tools to help global corporations develop brand strategy. Design firms often partner with a market research firm, and in many cases are provided with existing research reports about customer preferences or marketing segments.

Researchers use information to quantify, qualify, define, benchmark and cast a critical eye on a company and its brands, the markets they serve and the opportunities they seek.

Dennis Dunn, Ph.D., principal, B2BPulse

Qualitative research

The aim of qualitative research is to get insight into customer beliefs, feelings, and motives. Findings are often rich in context and may provide new insights and perspectives into purchasing decisions. Researchers use qualitative surveys usually as a prelude to large-scale quantitative studies.

Quantitative research

The aim of quantitative research is to provide enough information from enough different people to allow companies to predict—with an acceptable range of confidence—what might happen. A large group of people is asked exactly the same questions in precisely the same way. The sample is a microcosm that has the same characteristics of the overall target market. Researchers attempt to project the opinions of a relatively small number of people (the sample) to model the opinions of the entire population.

One-on-one interviews

These are individual in-depth interviews that are ideally conducted face to face. This method is effective with senior management, important customers, and thought leaders. Although it may be very expensive to send an interviewer out in the field to meet one on one with a respondent, the information this method yields is particularly valuable in terms of depth and context.

Online surveys

An online survey is one of several ways to gather primary research data. This approach uses the Internet to gather information from respondents as they sit at their own computers. Typically, potential respondents receive an e-mail that invites them to take a survey. The e-mail contains a link that respondents can click to take them to a web page where they complete the survey.

Focus groups

A focus group, a type of qualitative research, is built around a fast-paced meeting with seven to ten participants who are carefully selected because they share common characteristics. The group meets for about two hours to discuss predetermined topics introduced by the discussion leader or facilitator. Focus groups are considered valuable because they stimulate thoughts and discussions that are not possible with other types of research. Focus groups are best used to discover attitudes, perceptions, needs, prejudices, ways of using products, and viewpoints on pricing and distribution.

Eye tracking

Eye movement recorders examine how an individual views packaging, advertisements, signs, shelf displays, or computer screens. The devices record eye movements. They show when the subject starts to view a picture, the order in which the elements of the image were examined and reexamined, and the amount of viewing time given each element.

Mystery shopping

Trained mystery shoppers anonymously visit stores, branch banks, and other locations where they pose as customers. They evaluate the shopping experience, salesmanship, professionalism, closing skills, follow-up, and overall satisfaction. Mystery shoppers follow a list of predefined steps, make mental notes, observe conditions and performance, and produce audit reports that provide objective feedback to management.

Usability testing

This type of testing examines how easily users navigate a website. Teams that consist of designers and human-factor engineers observe a user through a two-way mirror in a formal laboratory testing environment. Users are selected carefully, and results are analyzed in depth. Informal usability testing takes place in an individual's work environment and may not include human-factor engineers.

Segmentation

Consumers and businesses are divided into clustered groups, each with its own special interests, lifestyles, and affinity for particular goods and services. Consumer segments are usually defined by demographic and psychographic information. Demographics are vital statistics such as age, sex, marital status, ethnicity, family size and composition, education, income, occupation, and housing. Psychographics refer to psychological attributes that describe an individual's lifestyle or attitudes. Business segments are often described in terms of the nature or size of the business. Variables such as industry, geographic scope, number of employees, dollar volume, and types of customers served are important.

Global segmentation

Geography, culture, and language are segmentation variables just like industry, occupation, gender, income, education, and marital status. As companies become global, the need to understand customer needs, wants, expectations and behaviors becomes more complex. Language, cultural perspectives, and value systems differ dramatically. Concepts and approaches that work well in the United States may fail miserably in Saudi Arabia, France, or Japan.

Insight into the characteristics, needs, and perceptions of the target customer and other stakeholders is critical to defining a brand strategy and, ultimately, designing an effective identity. Stakeholders refer to various constituencies that may affect the future of an enterprise. The most pivotal and revealing question to ask a CEO or a founder of a new company is "How do you want to be perceived by your various stakeholders?" Through understanding the needs of the customers, designers develop solutions that are appropriate and compelling.

Apple's "Switch" advertising campaign, designed by TBWA Chiat Day, targets PC users—from the technologically astute to the frustrated neophyte. Apple seizes every opportunity from marketing through product design to convey to its customers that it understands their needs, challenges, and aspirations.

We hope our SoHo store will surprise and delight both Mac and PC users who want to see everything the Mac can do to enhance their digital lifestyles.

Steve Jobs, CEO
Apple Computer

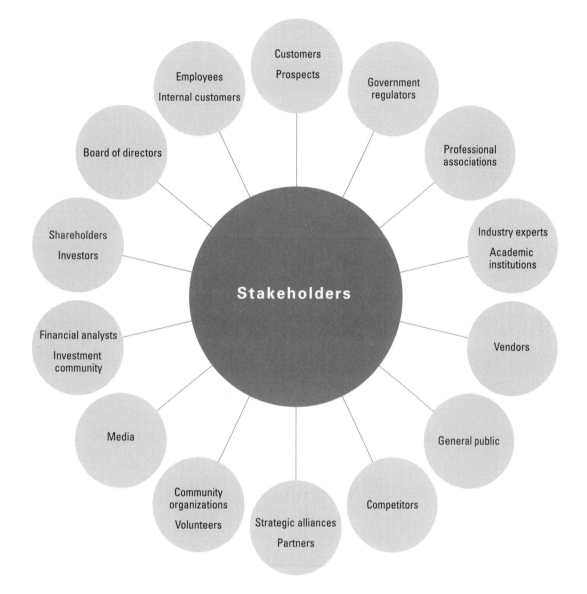

Stakeholders

- Customers / Prospects
- Government regulators
- Professional associations
- Industry experts / Academic institutions
- Vendors
- General public
- Competitors
- Strategic alliances / Partners
- Community organizations / Volunteers
- Media
- Financial analysts / Investment community
- Shareholders / Investors
- Board of directors
- Employees / Internal customers

Apple's logo, designed in 1977, is an apple with a bite out of it—a friendly symbol of both knowledge and anarchy, contrasted to IBM and the PC world.

If you want to build a brand, you must focus your branding efforts on owning a word in the prospect's mind. A word that no one else owns. What prestige is to Mercedes, safety is to Volvo.

Al Ries and Laura Ries, co-authors, *The 22 Immutable Laws of Branding*

The greater the insight into the competition, the greater the competitive edge. Differentiating a company from its leading competitors is critical. Positioning the company in relationship to the competition is both a marketing and design challenge. "Why should the customer choose our products or services over others?" is the marketing challenge. "We need to look and feel different" is the design imperative.

A competitive audit is a dynamic, data-gathering process. Simply put, this audit examines the competition's brands, their key messages, and their identity in the marketplace, from their brandmarks and taglines, to their ads and websites. More than ever, it's easy to gather information on the Internet; however, one should not stop there. Finding ways to experience the competition as a customer often provides valuable insights.

The breadth and depth of this audit can vary widely depending on the nature of the company and the scope of the project. Frequently, a company has its own competitive intelligence—qualitative or quantitative research that can be a source of critical data that need to be reviewed. Occasionally, proprietary research will be conducted during this task.

Observe, listen, document, analyze

The competitive audit process

Identify competitors	*Gather information/ research*	*Determine positioning*	*Identify key messages*	*Examine visual identity*
Who are leading competitors?	List information needed	Examine competitive positioning	Mission	Symbols
Who most closely resembles the client, and in what ways?	Examine existing research and materials	Identify features/benefits	Tagline	Meaning
Which companies compete indirectly?	Determine if additional research is required	Identity strengths/ weaknesses	Descriptors	Shape
	Consider interviews, focus groups, online surveys	Examine brand personality	Themes from advertising and collaterals	Color
				Typography

Understanding the competition

Who are they?

What do their brands stand for?

What markets/audiences do they serve?

What advantages (strengths) do they have?

What disadvantages (weaknesses) do they have?

What are their modes of selling and cultivating customers/clients?

How do they position themselves?

How do they characterize their customers/clients?

What are their key messages?

What is their financial condition?

How much market share do they hold?

How does the competition use brand identity to leverage success?

What do they look and feel like?

Using the Competitive Audit

Present audit at the end of the planning and analysis phase

Use learnings to develop new brand and positioning strategy

Use audit to inform the design process

Consider meaning, shape, color, form, and content that the competition does not use

Use audit when presenting new brand identity strategies to demonstrate differentiation

A competitive audit for a marketing research firm.

Document identity	**Examine naming strategy**	**Examine brand hierarchy**	**Experience the competition**	**Synthesize learnings**
Identity signatures	Core brand name	What type of brand architecture?	Navigate websites	Make conclusions
Marketing collateral materials + website	Naming system for products and services	How integrated or independent is the core brand in relation to subsidiaries or subbrands?	Visit shops and offices	Start seeing opportunities
Sales and promotional tools	Descriptors and domains		Purchase and use products	Organize presentation
Brand architecture		How are the products and services organized?	Use services	
Signage			Listen to a sales pitch	
			Call customer service	

Repositioning an organization, revitalizing and redesigning an existing identity system, or developing a new identity for a merger requires an examination of the communications and marketing tools an organization has used in the past. Determining what has worked and what has been less successful or even dysfunctional provides valuable learnings in the creation of a new identity. Mergers present the most challenging audit scenarios because two companies that were competitors are now becoming aligned.

The purpose of an internal audit is to methodically examine and analyze all marketing, communications, and identity systems, both existing and those out of circulation. Sometimes referred to as the marketing or perceptual audit, the process takes a magnifying glass to the brand and its multiple expressions over time. To develop a vision for an organization's brand in the future, one must have a sense of its history.

Inevitably, something of worth has been tossed out over time—a tagline, a symbol, a phrase, a point of view—for what seemed to be a good reason at the time. There might be something from the past that should be resuscitated or repurposed. Perhaps there's a color or a tagline that has been in place since the founding of the company—consider whether this equity should be moved forward.

Gather, review, analyze, document

Methods of organizing audits

Create a war room and put everything on the walls.

Buy file boxes and create hanging files for categories.

Devise a standard system to capture findings.

Take a "before" picture.

The internal audit process

Understand	*Request materials*	*Create a system*	*Solicit information*
Markets served	Provide detailed list:	Organization	Contextual/historical background
Sales + distribution	Existing materials	Retrieval	Marketing management
Marketing management	Archival materials	Documentation	Communications functions
Communications functions		Review	Attitudes toward brand
Internal technology			Attitudes toward identity

Request materials

The following is the broad range of materials to request. It's important to create an effective organization and retrieval system, since in all probability you will be amassing a large collection. It's important to have someone provide some background information about what has worked and what hasn't from a brand identity perspective.

Determine how things get done that relate to communications, marketing, and design for insight into what kind of brand identity system to build.

Brand identity

All versions of all identities ever used

All signatures, marks, logotypes

Company names

Division names

Product names

All taglines

All trademarks owned

Standards and guidelines

Business papers

Letterhead, envelopes, labels, business cards

Fax forms

Invoices, statements

Proposal covers

Folders

Forms

Electronic communications

Website

Intranet

Extranet

Videos

Sales and marketing

Sales and product literature

Newsletters

Advertising campaigns

Investor relations materials

Annual reports

Seminar literature

PowerPoint presentations

Internal communications, miscellaneous

Employee communications

Ephemera (T-shirts, baseball caps, pens)

Holiday greetings

Environmental applications

External signage

Internal signage

Store interiors

Banners

Trade show booths

Retail

Packaging

Promotions

Shopping bags

Menus

Merchandise

Displays

Examine materials

- Brand identity
- Business papers
- Electronic communications
- Sales + marketing
- Internal communications
- Environmental
- Retail

Examine use of identity

- Marks
- Logotypes
- Color
- Imagery
- Typography

Examine how things happen

- Communications responsibility
- In-house design department
- Advertising agency
- Printing
- Webmaster, etc.

Document learnings

- Equity
- Brand architecture
- Positioning
- Key messages
- Visual language

Clarifying brand strategy involves both methodical examination and strategic imagination. It's not unlike looking into a microscope with one eye and a telescope with the other. This phase is about analysis, discovery, synthesis, simplicity, and clarity. This combination of rational thinking and creative intelligence characterizes the best strategies, which go where others have not.

In Phase 2, all of the learnings from Phase I are distilled into a unifying idea and a positioning strategy. Agreement is solidified about target markets, competitive advantage, brand core values, brand attributes, and project goals. More often than not, the definitions of the problem and its challenges have evolved. Although many companies have their values and attributes in place, they may not have taken the time to articulate and refine them, or to share them beyond an offsite management retreat. The role of the consultant here is to identify, articulate, illuminate, weave, and play back the possibilities.

Phase 2 can lead to a number of possible outcomes. In a merger, a new brand strategy for the combined enterprise is necessary. Other scenarios require a unifying idea that will be effective across business lines in a new brand identity program. A brand brief is created and a discussion about findings and epiphanies follows. When there is openness and candor between the client and the consultant, true collaboration can produce the exceptional. Key success factors during this phase are trust and mutual respect.

The client is the author. We are the interpreter.

Bart Crosby, principal, Crosby Associates

Phase 2 scenarios

There are at least three different scenarios in branding projects that determine the scope of services during the second phase.

1

A clearly defined brand strategy exists.

When Turner Duckworth worked with Amazon.com and Jeff Bezos, brand strategy was already clearly defined and articulated. What Amazon needed was a world class brand identity. When Sandstrom Design was brought in by Steve Sandoz, a creative director at Weiden Kennedy, to work on TAZO tea, a vision that was articulated as "Marco Polo meets Merlin" was already in place. What the TAZO team needed was a firm that knew how to design the product offering and render it "otherworldly." When Bernhardt Fudyma worked with Nabisco to evaluate its familiar red triangle trademark design, the firm conducted an in-depth evaluation process, which did not require strategy development.

2

A need to redefine brand strategy.

When Harley-Davidson set out to turn around its business and reinvent itself, senior leadership decided to build a brand strategy based on existing rider passion. Over the years, they worked collaboratively with David Aaker, a preeminent brand strategist, as well as their agencies, VSA Partners and Carmichael Lynch, to evolve and express their strategy. When the Tate in the U.K. wanted to enhance its appeal and attract more visitors to their four museums, Sir Nicholas Serota, the Tate's director and his communications staff, worked closely with Wolff Olins to develop a central brand idea that would unify the different museums. "Look again, think again," was an invitation to visitors to reconsider their experience of art.

3

A need to create brand strategy.

Mergers are by far the most challenging scenarios that require new brand strategy. Determining a unified strategy and a new name for two companies that may have been competitors, and working with a transition team in a compressed timeframe, takes extraordinary skill and diplomacy. VSA Partners created a brand strategy and a new name, Cingular, for the joint venture of Bell South Mobility and SBC Wireless in six weeks. The new name would represent eleven former brands and over 21 million customers. The brand strategy positioned Cingular as the embodiment of human expression, since VSA viewed the wireless space evolving from a features-and-functions buying decision to a lifestyle choice.

1. Revisit the vision

Interviews with senior management, employees, customers, and industry experts provide an intimate glance into the uniqueness of a company. If one is lucky, the CEO is a visionary who has a clear picture of an ideal future and all its possibilities. Often, such visionaries are hard to find. It is important to look for the gold— sometimes a business is so busy servicing its customers, that it has forgotten the core ideas around why it is so successful. Sometimes it takes a customer's loyalty and clarity to bring it back. Sometimes, listening to a sales presentation by the company's most successful rep provides valuable insight.

2. Look at the really big picture

It's never enough to examine a company's business strategy, core values, target markets, competitors, distribution channels, technology, and competitive advantage. It's important to stand back and look at trends that are affecting the future, whether they are economic, socio-political, global, or lifestyle. It's important to observe other brands outside of the industry sector, and how they express their brand strategy. It's important, in the case of a more mature company, to look back historically and to take note of what the drivers have been that have made this company successful.

3. Engage in meaningful dialogue

It's so easy to be caught up in daily tasks, that companies frequently do not take the time to revisit who they are and what they are about. The beauty of this process is that it gives senior managers an explicit reason to go off-site and spin a dream. It's a worthwhile exercise, even if off-site turns out to be just the conference room with no calls and no distractions. Superb consultants know how to facilitate a dialogue between core leaders in which various brand scenarios are explored and brand attributes surface.

A brand becomes stronger when you narrow the focus.

Al Ries and Laura Ries, co-authors, The 22 Immutable Laws of Branding

As the mass and volume of information increases, people search for a clear signal—one who gives pattern, shape, direction to the voice.

Bruce Mau, designer

4. Uncover brand essence (or simple truth)

What does a company do that is best in world? Why do their customers choose them over their competition? What business are they in? How are they really different than their most successful competitor? What are three adjectives that summarize how this company wants to be perceived? What are their strengths and weaknesses? The clarity of these answers is an important driver in this phase.

5. Develop a positioning platform

Subsequent to information gathering and analysis is the development and refinement of a positioning strategy. Perceptual mapping is frequently a technique that used to brainstorm a positioning strategy. On what dimension can a company compete? What can it own? Where can it go that is different from the competition?

6. Create the big idea

The big idea can always be expressed in one sentence, although the rationale could usually fill a book. Sometimes the big idea becomes the tagline or the battle cry (like Think Different.), and sometimes it's purely aspirational. The big idea must be simple and transportable—it must carry enough ambiguity to allow for future developments that cannot be predicted. It must create an emotional connection and it must be easy to talk about, whether you are the CEO or an employee.

7. Play it back

Sometimes old ideas that are framed in a new way don't resonate immediately. The consultant needs to hold up a mirror and say, "This is what you have told me and I heard it again from your customers and your sales force. And this is why it is powerful."

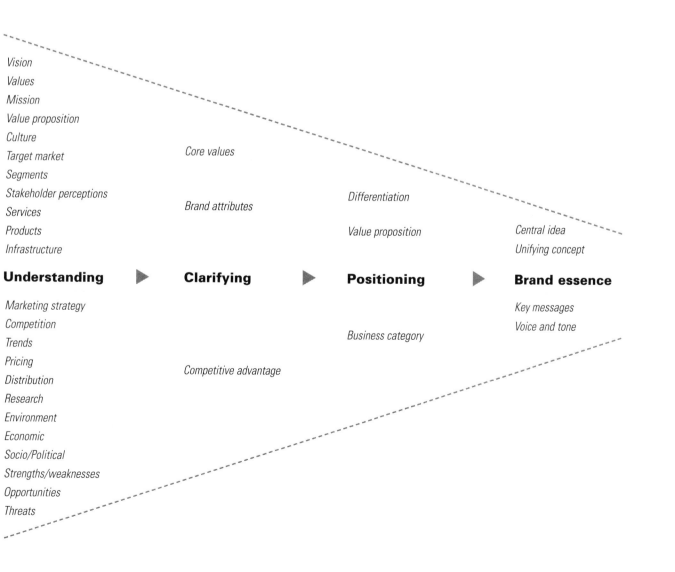

Vision
Values
Mission
Value proposition
Culture
Target market
Segments
Stakeholder perceptions
Services
Products
Infrastructure

Core values

Brand attributes

Differentiation

Value proposition

Central idea
Unifying concept

Understanding ▶ **Clarifying** ▶ **Positioning** ▶ **Brand essence**

Marketing strategy
Competition
Trends
Pricing
Distribution
Research
Environment
Economic
Socio/Political
Strengths/weaknesses
Opportunities
Threats

Competitive advantage

Business category

Key messages
Voice and tone

Articulating a company's core values, its mission or its brand attributes would appear to be a fairly simple exercise for the leadership of an organization. It is actually a difficult and strategic process characterized by extensive dialogue. A skilled facilitator, experienced in building consensus and getting closure, is needed to ask the right questions. The result of this work is a critical component in the realization of a compelling brand strategy and a differentiated brand identity.

The best "statements" are simply worded, and function as an organizational totem pole around which behavior, actions, and communications are aligned. They may be used internally as an affirmation of a distinctive culture and externally as a competitive advantage. They are a springboard for responsible creative work (thinking, designing, naming) or a litmus test against which success is measured. Following are some examples of how some organizations express their brand attributes, brand values, principles or big ideas. The simplicity of the language is so deceptive, because the process getting there is inevitably complex.

A successful brand is all about detail. Every facet of a brand must be apparent in an organization's communications, behavior, products and environment.

Brian Boylan, chairman,
Wolff Olins

Citi

Michael Wolff, a brand strategist who worked with Citicorp and Travelers after the merger described a compelling brand strategy for the future by saying, "We want to become the bank of the future. We really need to imagine talking to our two billionth customer. She is an eleven-year-old girl named Melissa. She thinks of banking services in a whole new way, grows up doing all of her banking on line, and expects everything to be simple. She lives in the world of McDonald's, Nike, the Gap, and Coke." Wolff and the Pentagram team wanted to reduce the brandname to Citi, and showed Melissa and Citi in a field of super brands.

Big Ideas

A tagline can distill the essence of a brand.

Apple
Think different

Target
Pay less. Expect more.

eBay
The world's online marketplace

Saturn
A different kind of car company

TAZO
The reincarnation of tea

FedEx
The world on time

A single word

Sometimes a single word can capture the brand essence.

Volvo = Safety

Mercedes = Prestige

Chicago GSB

Chicago GSB is the University of Chicago Graduate School of Business. Its mission is to "produce ideas, thinkers, and leaders who change the practice of business." Its promise to its students is "With a Chicago degree, you, too, will lead and transform business." The following brand attributes were created with the assistance of Crosby Associates as part of the branding process.

World-Class

Intelligent

Prestigious

Proud

Individualistic

Smart

Resourceful

Rigorous

Innovative

Analytical

Passionate

Ambitious

Having tradition

FedEx

Landor Associates worked with FedEx brand leaders to update core brand attributes, which supported the future vision. The attributes are relevant across a broad spectrum of transportation and logistics services.

Simplifying
It's easy to work with FedEx. We don't waste anyone's time. Our procedures are straightforward, and our communications are clear.

Optimizing
Every FedEx customer has different needs. We find the right solution and the right price—for each customer's business.

Certain
Our customers don't have time for "almost." They demand certainty. FedEx delivers.

Personal
FedEx customers are people, not transactions. We get to know each customer and offer him or her the tools they need to achieve their goals.

Inventive
Global business constantly changes. So does FedEx. As we invent new solutions, we lead the way in operations, technology, and e-commerce.

Connecting
FedEx makes connections. Our networks link people, packages, and information around the clock and around the world.

Please refer to case study section for more information on Citi, Chicago GSB, and FedEx.

The brief is both an end and a beginning. Research and analysis is complete, project goals have evolved, and there is clarity around target markets, and positioning. Everyone is ready to ignite the creative process that will result in a new name perhaps, a repositioned brand or an integrated and unified global identity program. The brief provides an opportunity for the client to reaffirm the fundamental premises of the brand strategy, and to give the go ahead to proceed. The brief routinely engenders a robust conversation, especially when the research and analysis has produced some keen insights or epiphanies.

Various firms call this presentation by different names—from "brand positioning" to "creative brief." It doesn't matter what it is called. What matters is that all decision makers are present and that they all agree on unified goals, positioning, and strategy prior to seeing any brand identity solutions.

The brief is usually presented in a meeting and may be handed out as a document after the presentation. The meeting is an opportunity to engage in meaningful dialogue with key decision makers and to build trust in the evolution of the brand identity. Consensus building and momentum start here. Frequently, key beliefs about branding and brand identity are also woven into this presentation. The depth and breadth of this presentation are directly related to the complexity and nature of the engagement and the amount of research that has been conducted. Some firms, like Turner Duckworth, provide their clients with a brand questionnaire and the clients respond with a brief that guides the creative process.

Characteristics of the best briefs

Succinct

Strategic

Relevant

Value-added

Actionable

Elements of the brief

Review of process to date
This is a short summary of what has been accomplished to date and may include orientation, information gathering, communications and competitive audits, review of strategic documents and history, other brand research, interviews, site visits, and evaluation.

Industry trends
A review of the factors that are affecting the future success of the company and key constituencies.

Key stakeholders
A list of stakeholders, their needs, and how the company needs to be perceived by each group.

Internal audit
Analysis and presentation of existing brand, name, brand identity systems, brand equity, and marketing tools. May include all names, visual identities, and taglines to date. In the case of a merger, all merged companies are showcased.

Competitive audit
Conclusions are presented that describe how key competitors are positioning themselves. It's important to demonstrate different brand and marketing strategies, including naming, marks, taglines, and various applications, as well as brand architecture strategies.

Interview findings
Frequently, excerpts from interviews are presented to senior management that provides insight into the essence of the brand. Excerpts are presented either in stakeholder categories or in other categories that are thematic.

Research findings
If proprietary market research has been conducted, slides are included that demonstrate levels of brand awareness vis-a-vis competitors, and testing of various perceptual factors and consumer needs. If the identity firm was provided with existing research, key relevant learnings are summarized from the reports.

Brand architecture
A chart may be shown that demonstrates the relationships of the various existing brands and subbrands in the case of an existing company or a merger. It may be shown in a before-and-after format.

Brand attributes
A list of adjectives describes the ideal tone, positioning, and personality of the company and its brand. Identity firms distill adjectives from senior management interviews and documents, which are then used in the creative process to drive the development of the brand identity. Attributes are primarily used to describe the brand.

Brand strategy
The brand strategy defines positioning, differentiation, the competitive advantage, and a unique value proposition. Brand strategy should demonstrate how the brand could translate throughout all facets of the organization, from communications, behavior, and products through environment. If the project does not require a new brand strategy, the brand brief should repeat the existing strategy.

Goals
This list starts with positioning goals, brand attributes, and value propositions, and follows with specific brand identity goals for naming, brand architecture, and visual identity. Pragmatic constraints (sometimes called performance criteria) and challenges need to be listed as well.

Closure and next steps
There must be agreement on strategy, positioning, goals, and next steps. The most successful firms keep the ball in the air and provide a road map that includes scheduling and benchmarks.

Naming is a complex, creative, and iterative process that requires experience in linguistics, marketing, research, and trademark law. Naming is not for the weak of heart. Out of all the ideal qualities of an effective name—meaningful, memorable, future-oriented, protectable, visual, and positive—creating a brand name that can be legally protected presents the most formidable challenge, even for the experts.

Numerous brainstorming techniques are used to develop hundreds if not thousands of names, in order to produce a short list of viable names. Culling down the large list takes skill and patience. All names need to be judged against the performance criteria of an effective name, and against positioning and strategic goals as well. Equally challenging is getting a company to agree on a new name. It is difficult to understand that meaning and associations are built over time. Clients want to fall in love with a name as soon as they hear it. Agreement is not easy to achieve, especially when the choices seem limited. Some companies invest in extensive testing of the name in the target markets to test perceptions and to uncover any red flags—any negative connotations to the name.

The naming process

Revisit positioning	*Get organized*	*Create naming criteria*	*Brainstorm*
Examine brand goals and target market needs	Develop timeline	Performance criteria	Create numerous names
Evaluate existing names	Determine team	Positioning criteria	Organize in categories and themes
Examine competitor names	Finalize brainstorming techniques	Legal criteria	Look at hybrids and mimetics
	Determine search mechanisms	Regulatory criteria, if any	Be prolific
	Develop decision-making process		Explore variations/iterations on a theme
	Organize reference resources		

Inspiration

Language

Meaning

Personality

Dictionaries

Thesauruses

Latin

Greek

Foreign languages

Mass culture

Poetry

Television

Music

History

Art

Commerce

Colors

Symbols

Metaphors

Analogies

Sounds

Science

Technology

Astronomy

Myths

Stories

Values

Dreams

Most Prevalent Languages

English

Spanish

Russian

Japanese

Indonesian

Arabic

Bengali

Hindustani

Mandarin

Naming Basics

1 Brand names are valuable assets.

2 When you are brainstorming, there are no stupid ideas.

3 Always examine a name in context.

4 Consider sound, cadence, and how easy a name is to pronounce.

5 Be methodical in tracking name selections.

6 Determine smartest searching techniques.

7 Review all the criteria before you toss a name.

Naming Trivia

Although only 934,000 names are registered, there are over 20 million .com domains registered in 2002.

Remember

Names may be registered in different classes of goods and services.

Initial screening

- Positioning
- Linguistic
- Legal
- Common-law databases
- Online search engines
- Online phone directories
- Domain registration
- Create a short list

Contextual testing

- Say the name
- Leave a voice mail
- E-mail the name
- Put it in a business card
- Put it in an ad headline

Testing

- Determine methods to trust
- Check for red flags
- Unearth trademark conflicts
- Check language connotations
- Check cultural connotations
- Linguistic analysis

Final legal screen

- Domestic
- International
- Domain
- Regulatory
- Registration

Investigation and analysis are complete; the brand brief has been agreed upon, and the creative design process begins. Design is an iterative process that seeks to integrate meaning with form. The best designers work at the intersection of strategic imagination, intuition, design excellence, and experience. Reducing a complex idea to its visual essence requires skill, focus, patience, and unending discipline. A designer may examine hundreds of ideas before focusing on a final choice. Even after a final idea emerges, testing its viability begins yet another round of exploration. It is an enormous responsibility to design something that in all probability will be reproduced hundreds of thousands if not millions of times and has a lifetime of twenty years or more.

Creativity takes many roads. In some offices, numerous designers work on the same idea, whereas in other offices each designer might develop a different idea or positioning strategy. Routinely, hundreds of sketches are put up on the wall for a group discussion. Each preliminary approach can be a catalyst to a new approach. It is difficult to create a simple form that is bold, memorable, and appropriate because we live in an oversaturated visual environment, making it critical to ensure that the solution is unique and differentiated. In addition, an identity will need to be a workhorse across various media and applications.

In projects that involve redesign, the designer must also carefully examine the equity of the existing form and understand what it has meant to a company's culture. Paul Rand's logos for UPS, Westinghouse, and Cummins were all redesigns. In each case, Rand's genius was finding a way to maintain elements from the original identity and transform them into bigger ideas and stronger, more sustainable visual forms. His strategy was always to present one idea. His brilliant design sensibility was matched by his strategic presentations, in which he would trace the evolution of his recommendation.

Brinker Capital mark evolution:
Rev Group

The core idea evolved from
Brinker Capital's asset
management excellence.

A designer's perspective

Paul Rand, as excerpted from *Paul Rand* by Steven Heller

A logo is more important in a certain sense than a painting because a zillion people see the logo and it affects what they do. . . it affects everything. [Rand said]

Rand did not foresee the animated potential of the [Westinghouse] logo when he first designed it, but the possibilities for bringing it to life soon became perfectly clear.

Rand designed logos for endurance. 'I think permanence is something you find out,' he once said. 'It isn't something you design for. You design for durability, for function, for usefulness, for rightness, for beauty. But permanence is up to God and time.'

Per Mollerup, *Marks of Excellence*

The study of trademarks has its roots in fields as diverse as anthropology, history, heraldry, psychology, marketing, semiotics, communication theory, and of course, graphic design.

Identification, description, and the creation of value are just some of the possible functions of a trademark.

Steff Geissbuhler Chermayeff & Geismar

We have run out of abstract, geometric marks and symbols, where an artificially adopted notion of growth, global business and aggressive, forward-moving technology becomes meaningless and overused, because it's everybody's strategy, mission, and positioning.

We have found that our audiences react much more directly and emotionally to recognizable symbols and cultural icons with clear connotations, characteristics, and qualities.

The trademark, although a most important key element, can never tell the whole story. At best it conveys one or two notions or aspects of the business. The identity has to be supported by a visual language and a vocabulary.

Hans-U. Allemann Allemann Almquist & Jones

We usually begin with very predictable and obvious ideas, but the beauty of the identity design process is that it is totally unpredictable. We never know what the process will reveal. I have been designing marks for 40 years, and the process still astonishes me.

The best identity designers have a strong understanding of how to communicate effectively through the use of signs and symbols, have a keen sense of form and letterforms, and an understanding of the history of design.

Malcolm Grear Malcolm Grear Designers

Form and counterform. Light and tension. Expanded meaning that is not exhausted at first glance. These are the things that fascinate me.

You need to know the enterprise inside and out.

Beyond mere legibility, we aspire to convey our client's essential nature through imagery that is strong, profound and elegant.

Examine

Meaning

Attributes

Acronyms

Inspiration

History

Form

Counterform

Abstract

Pictorial

Letterform

Wordmark

Combination

Time

Space

Light

Still

Motion

Transition

Perspective

Reality

Fantasy

Straight

Curve

Angle

Intersection

Patterns

A logotype is a word (or words) in a determined font, which may be standard, modified, or entirely redrawn. Frequently, a logotype is juxtaposed to a symbol in a formal relationship called the signature. Logotypes not only need to be distinctive, but also need to be durable and sustainable. Legibility at various scales and in a range of media is imperative, whether a logotype is silk-screened on the side of a ballpoint pen or illuminated in an external sign twenty stories off the ground.

The best logotypes are a result of a careful typographic exploration. Designers consider the attributes of each letterform as well as the relationships between letterforms. In the best logotypes, letterforms may be redrawn, modified, and manipulated in order to express the appropriate personality and positioning of the company.

The designer begins her process by examining hundreds of typographic variations. Beginning with the basics—for example, whether the name should be set in all caps or caps and lowercase—the designer proceeds to look at classic and modern typefaces, roman and italic variations, and various weights, scales, and combinations. The designer then proceeds to manipulate and customize the logotype. Each decision is driven by visual and performance considerations as well as by what the typography itself communicates.

A signature is the specific and non-negotiable designed combination of the brandmark and the logotype.The best signatures have specific isolation zones to protect their presence. A company may have numerous signatures—for various business lines or with and without a tagline.

The Wharton identity program, designed by Joel Katz Design Associates, features the word "Wharton" set in a distinctive type treatment. The letterforms, including the "Wh" ligature, were redrawn and reproportioned. The logotype exists in two versions: "large" for use at sizes larger than 1/2" high, and "small" for use at 1/2" and smaller. A number of signatures were created, including logotype and tagline signatures, division and program signatures, and joint venture signatures. The following is excerpted from Wharton's identity manual and style guide.

Logotype and Tagline Signature

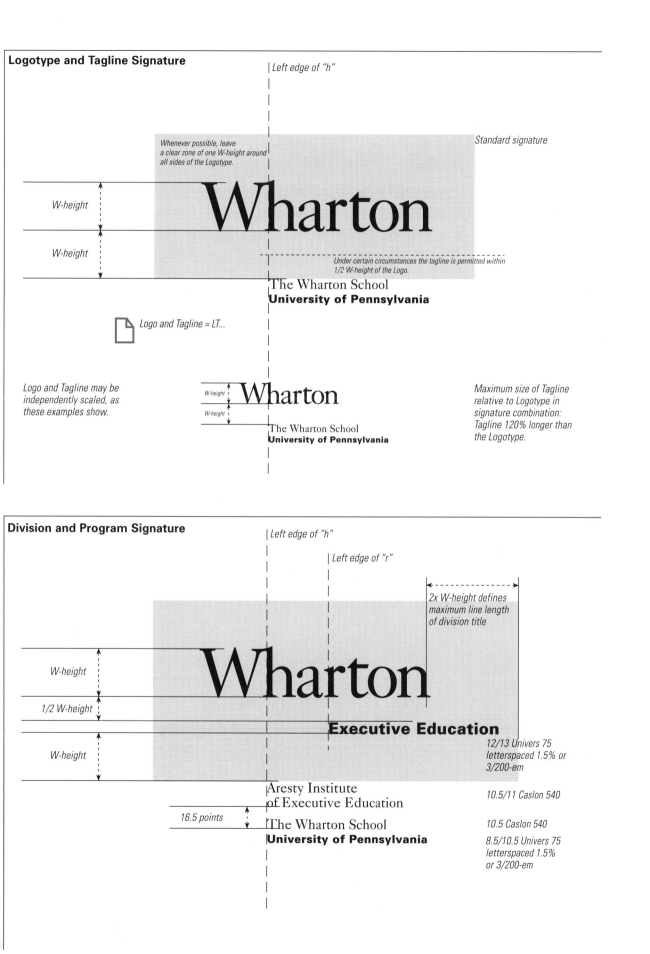

Left edge of "h"

Whenever possible, leave a clear zone of one W-height around all sides of the Logotype.

Standard signature

W-height

W-height

Wharton

Under certain circumstances the tagline is permitted within 1/2 W-height of the Logo.

The Wharton School
University of Pennsylvania

Logo and Tagline = LT...

Logo and Tagline may be independently scaled, as these examples show.

W-height
W-height

Wharton

The Wharton School
University of Pennsylvania

Maximum size of Tagline relative to Logotype in signature combination: Tagline 120% longer than the Logotype.

Division and Program Signature

Left edge of "h"

Left edge of "r"

2x W-height defines maximum line length of division title

W-height

1/2 W-height

W-height

Wharton

Executive Education

12/13 Univers 75 letterspaced 1.5% or 3/200-em

Aresty Institute of Executive Education

10.5/11 Caslon 540

16.5 points

The Wharton School

10.5 Caslon 540

University of Pennsylvania

8.5/10.5 Univers 75 letterspaced 1.5% or 3/200-em

A school bus by any another color is no longer a school bus. Its essence is expressed by the color yellow. As consumers, we depend on the familiarity of Coca-Cola cans that are red and UPS trucks that are brown. A person doesn't need to read the type on a Tiffany gift box in order to know where the gift was purchased. Tiffany's signature blue sets off a series of immediate impressions that are aligned with the company's overall positioning and brand identity strategy.

In the sequence of visual perception, the brain reads color after it registers a shape and before it reads content. Choosing a color for a new identity requires a core understanding of color theory, a clear vision of how the brand needs to be perceived and differentiated, and an ability to master consistency and meaning over a broad range of mediums.

Color is used to evoke emotion, express personality, and stimulate brand association. While some color is used to unify an identity, other colors may be used functionally to clarify brand architecture, through differentiating products or business lines. Designers formulate special and unique brand identity color strategies. Traditionally, the primary brand color is assigned to the symbol, and the secondary color is assigned to the logotype, business descriptor, or tagline. In addition to the core brand colors, system color palettes are developed to support a broad range of communications needs. Ensuring optimum reproduction of the brand color is an integral part of basic standards and part of the challenge as new media tools proliferate.

Color creates emotion, triggers memory, and gives sensation.

Gael Towey, creative director, Martha Stewart Living Omnimedia

Color brand identity basics

1 The ultimate goal is to own a color—a color that facilitates recognition and builds brand equity.

2 Different viewers experience color differently in various environments. The designer is the ultimate arbiter for setting consistency across platforms.

3 Ensuring consistency across multiple media is an enormous challenge, and there is no off-the-shelf solution.

4 Color is dramatically affected by various file formats and reproduction media. Test. Test. Test.

5 Remember, most of the world is on a PC and uses PowerPoint.

6 A commitment to quality reproduction and execution needs to be a top-down initiative in order to insure that the asset is protected.

7 Sixty percent of the decision to buy a product is based on color.

8 One can never know enough about color. Depend on your basic color theory knowledge: warm, cool, values, hues, tints, shades, complementary colors.

9 Develop the best tools to ensure the proper use of brand color.

10 Colors have different connotations in different cultures. Do your due diligence and research those markets and cultures.

11 Use color to build meaning and expand connotation.

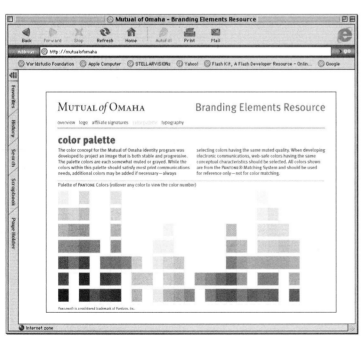

Mutual of Omaha branding resource website:
Crosby Associates

Testing the effectiveness of a color strategy

Is the color distinctive?

Is the color differentiated from competitors?

Is the color appropriate to the type of business?

Is the color aligned with brand strategy?

What do you want the color to communicate?

Will the color have sustainability?

What meaning have you assigned to the color?

Does the color have positive connotations in the target markets?

Does the color have positive or negative connotations in foreign markets?

Is the color reminiscent of any other product or service?

Will the color facilitate recognition and recall?

Did you consider a specially formulated color?

Can the color be legally protected?

Does the color work on white?

Can you reverse the mark out of black and still maintain the original intention?

What background colors are possible?

What background values are necessary?

How does scale affect the color?

When you have a one-color application such as a fax or the newspaper, how will you adjust the color so that it reads?

Are there technical challenges to getting the color right?

Can you achieve consistency across media?

Have you tested the color on a range of monitors, PC and Mac?

Have you looked at ink draws on coated and uncoated stock?

Have you considered that the PMS color may look dramatically different for coated and uncoated?

Will this color work in signage?

What are the color equivalents on the web?

Is there a vinyl binder color that is compatible?

Have you tested the color in the environment in which it will be used?

Have you created the appropriate color electronic files?

Color systems

Will the color system be flexible enough to allow for a range of dynamic applications?

Does the color system support a consistent experience of the brand?

Does the color system support the brand architecture?

Is the color system differentiated from that of the competition?

Have you examined the benefits and disadvantages of

  using color to differentiate products?

  using color to identify business lines?

  using colors to navigate decisions?

  using color to categorize information?

Do you need a bold palette and a pastel palette?

Can you reproduce these colors?

Have you developed a web palette and a print palette?

Have you named your colors?

Have you created identity standards that make it easy to use the color system?

Mergers, acquisitions, redesign

Have you examined the historical use of color?

Is there equity that should be preserved?

Is the color aligned with the new brand strategy?

Is there a symbolic color that communicates the positive outcome of the merged entities?

Will developing a new color for the company send a new and immediate signal about the future?

Will retiring an existing color confuse existing customers?

Color trivia

Kodak was the first company to trademark a signature color.

Bianchi created a special color green for their bicycles.

When British Petroleum and Amoco merged to form BP, British Petroleum's distinctive green and yellow colors were kept.

Our primary brand color is CIGNA teal. It is a specially formulated color that is unique to our industry. We want CIGNA to be strongly associated with CIGNA teal. Therefore, all businesses are encouraged to use this color broadly across their communications.

CIGNA Brand Identity Guidelines

Typography is a core building block of an effective identity program. Companies such as Apple, Mercedes-Benz, and Citibank are immediately recognizable in great part due to the distinctive and consistent typographical style that is used with intelligence and purpose throughout thousands of applications over time. A unified and coherent company image is not possible without typography that has a unique personality and an inherent legiblity. Typography must support the positioning strategy and information hierarchy. Identity program typography needs to be sustainable and not on the curve of a fad.

Thousands of fonts have been created by renowned typographers, designers, and type foundries over the centuries, and new typefaces are being created each day. Some identity firms routinely design a proprietary font for a client. Choosing the right font requires a basic knowledge of the breadth of options and a core understanding of how effective typography functions. Issues of functionality differ dramatically on a form, a pharmaceutical package, an ad in a magazine, and a website. The typeface needs to be flexible and easy to use, and must provide a wide range of expression. Clarity and legibility are the drivers.

Type is magical. It not only communicates a word's information, but it conveys a subliminal message.

Erik Spiekermann, author, Stop Stealing Sheep

Type trivia

Frutiger was designed for an airport.

Matthew Carter designed Bell Gothic to increase legibility in the phone book.

Meta was designed by Meta Design for the German post office but never used.

Wolff Olins designed Tate for Tate Modern in London.

Typeface family basics

1 Typefaces are chosen for their legibility, their unique character, and their range of weights and widths.

2 Intelligent typography supports information hierarchy.

3 Typeface families must be chosen to complement the signature, not necessarily to replicate the signature.

4 The best standards identify a range of fonts but give the users flexibility to choose the appropriate font, weight, and size for the message conveyed.

5 Limiting the number of fonts that a company uses is cost-effective, since licensing fonts is legally required.

6 The number of typeface families in a system is a matter of choice. Many companies choose serif and sans serif faces; some companies choose one font for everything.

7 Basic standards sometimes allow special display faces for unique situations.

8 The website may require its own set of typefaces and typography standards.

9 The best typographers examine a level of detail that includes numerals and bullets.

10 Many companies identify separate typefaces for internally produced word-processed documents and electronic presentations.

11 There are certain industries that have compliance requirements regarding type size for certain consumer products and communications.

Examine typefaces that:

1 Convey feeling and reflect positioning

2 Cover the range of application needs

3 Work in a range of sizes

4 Work in black and white and color

5 Differ from the competition's

6 Are compatible with the signature

7 Are legible

8 Have personality

9 Are sustainable

10 Reflect culture

Examine

Serif

Sans serif

Size

Weight

Curves

Rhythm

Descenders

Ascenders

Capitalization

Headlines

Subheads

Text

Titles

Callouts

Captions

Bulleted lists

Leading

Line length

Letter spacing

Numerals

Symbols

Quotation marks

The design of the core brand identity elements—i.e., the mark and the logotype—is only the beginning of the identity design process. Marks should not be shown to the client until rigorous testing and exploration of the concept's viablity is complete. From a design perspective, what may work in isolation may not meet the rigors of an entire system design. Seeing a signature out of context on a blank sheet of paper doesn't help sell—clients need to envision the possibilities.

Key applications that represent real future scenarios need to be identified. Frequently, these are outlined in a contractual agreement. A typical list for a small engagement might include a business card, a home page, an advertisement, a brochure cover, a letterhead, and something fun, like a baseball cap. On larger projects, the designer needs to demonstrate the effectiveness of brand extensions and the ability of the identity to work across business lines and markets served. In retail projects, the designer needs to explore how this identity would work within a retail environment and affect the customer experience.

Design exploration helps build a case for a particular design concept by demonstrating that it will support the marketing and communications needs of the company into the future. Flexibility, consistency, and sustainability are essential. The magic of an idea becomes real and easier to approve.

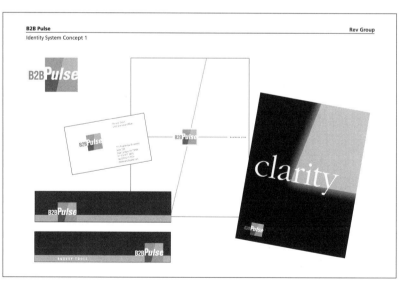

Presentation to B2BPulse market
research firm:
Rev Group

Testing the concept

Choose the most visible applications.

Choose the most challenging applications.

Examine the flexibility of the identity.

Examine how to express coherence and consistency.

Does the signature work?

Is it differentiated enough from the competition's?

Is it scalable?

Does it maintain impact?

Does it stay legible at a small scale?

Will it work in different media?

Will it work on the Internet?

Can it move?

Will it work both in color and in black and white?

Will it be conducive to brand extensions?

It works with the parent; will it work with the divisions?

Can it accommodate a tagline in the signature?

Will it work in other cultures?

Identity design testing basics

1   Use real scenarios and real text for application testing.

2   Continue asking the big questions in regard to appropriate meaning, sustainability, and flexibility.

3   Start thinking about the implications for the entire system of color and typeface families.

4   Always examine best-case and worst-case scenarios.

5   Remember—this is an iterative process.

6   If something doesn't work, deal with it immediately. Go back to the beginning if necessary to examine the core concept. Perhaps the signature needs to be reworked.

7   Date and assign a version number to the entire sketch process; be obsessive about organization of this phase.

8   Think ahead to production: how will this look on a screen? Test it on a PC.

9   Solicit feedback from trusted colleagues—designers and nondesigners—to reveal any connotations that may not be apparent.

10   Anticipate what you will need to present the design strategy; start envisioning the presentation.

11   Continue to actively think about the future: five and ten years out is sooner than you think.

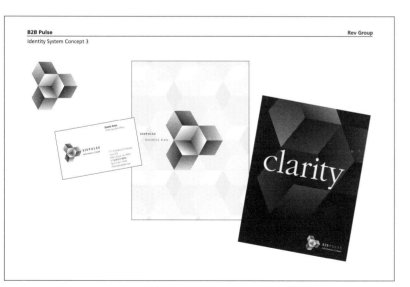

The first major design presentation is the decisive moment. A design team has worked hard to get to this point, and it is the culmination of months of work. The expectations and stakes are high. Clients are usually impatient during the planning and analysis phase since they are so focused on the end goal, which is their new brand identity. There is usually a sense of urgency around scheduling this meeting—everyone is ready to hit the ground running, even though the implementation phase of the work is not imminent.

Careful planning is essential to ensure the success of the outcome of the meeting. The smartest, most appropriate, and most creative solutions can get annihilated in a mismanaged presentation. The larger the group of decision makers, the more difficult the meeting and the decision are to manage. Even presenting to one decision maker alone demands planning in advance.

Delivering a good presentation is something that a professional learns through experience and observation. The best presentations stay focused on the agenda, keep the meeting moving within the scheduled time, set out clear and reasonable expectations, and are based on a decision-making process for making decisions that has been predetermined. The best presenters are well prepared and have practiced in advance. They are prepared to deal with any objections and can discuss the design solutions strategically, aligning them with the overall brand goals of the company. Larger projects routinely involve more than one presentation and numerous levels of building consensus.

Don't expect the work to speak for itself. Even the most ingenious solutions must be sold.

Suzanne Young, communications strategist

Presentation basics

1 Agree in advance about the agenda and the decision-making process.

2 Clarify who will attend the meeting and the role they will play. Individuals who have not participated in the early part of the process may derail the process.

3 Circulate the agenda in advance. Be sure to include the overall goals of the meeting.

4 Create an in-depth outline of your presentation and practice in advance. Create a handout if appropriate.

5 Look at the room's physical layout in advance to decide where you want to present from and where you want others to sit.

6 Arrive well in advance to set up the room and be there to greet all the attendees.

7 If the company is going to provide any equipment for the meeting, test it in advance. Familiarize yourself with the lighting and temperature control in the room.

Presentation strategies

1 Begin the meeting with a review of the decisions made to date, including overall brand identity goals, definition of target audience, and positioning statement.

2 Present each approach as a strategy with a unique positioning concept. Talk about meaning, not aesthetics. Each strategy should be presented within several actual contexts (ad, home page, business card, etc.), as well as juxtaposed to the competition.

3 Always have a point of view. When presenting numerous solutions (never more than three), be ready to explain which one you would choose and why.

4 Be prepared to deal with objections—steer the conversation away from aesthetic criticism and toward functional and marketing criteria.

5 Never present anything that you don't believe in.

6 Never allow voting.

7 Be prepared to present next steps, including design development, trademarking, and application design.

8 Follow up the presentation with a memo outlining all decisions that were made.

The brand identity design concept has been approved, and a sense of urgency generates a fusillade of questions: "When we will get business cards?" followed by "How soon can we get our standards online?" Now that the major decisions have been made, most companies want to hit the ground running. The challenge to the identity firm is to keep the momentum going while ensuring that critical details are finalized.

Phase 4 is about design refinement and design development. In Phase 3, hypothetical applications were designed in order to test the ideas, and also to help sell the core concepts. The highest priority now is to refine and finalize the elements of the identity and to create signatures. This work requires an obsessive attention to detail—the files created are permanent. Final testing of the signature(s) in a variety of sizes and media is critical. Decisions around typeface families, color palettes, and secondary visual elements are finalized during this phase.

While the design team is fine-tuning, the company is organizing its final list of applications that need to be designed and produced. Core applications are prioritized, and content is either provided or developed. The intellectual property firm begins the trademark process, confirming what needs to be registered and in which industry classes. The lawyers confirm that there are no conflicting marks.

A brand identity program encompasses a unique visual language that will express itself across all applications. Regardless of the medium, the applications need to work in harmony. The challenge is to design the right balance between flexibility of expression and consistency in communications.

Design is intelligence made visible.

Lou Danziger, designer and educator

Application design essentials

1 Convey the brand personality.

2 Align with positioning strategy.

3 Create a point of view and a look and feel.

4 Make it work across all media.

5 Demonstrate understanding of the target customer.

6 Differentiate. Differentiate. Differentiate.

Design development basics

1 Design is an iterative process between the big picture and minutiae.

2 Designing real applications and the identity system are simultaneous.

3 Ensure that all assumptions are achievable.

4 Be open to additional discovery as it gets more real.

5 God is in the details.

Application design imperatives

Seize every opportunity to manage perception.

Create a unified visual language.

Start thinking about launch strategy.

Create balance between consistency and flexibility.

Produce real applications before finalizing standards.

Work on the highest-visibility applications first.

Know when to identify outside experts for collaboration.

Use spreadsheets to keep track of numerous applications.

Never show any application without showing alignment with brand strategy.

Be obsessive about quality.

Gather notes during this phase for standards and guidelines.

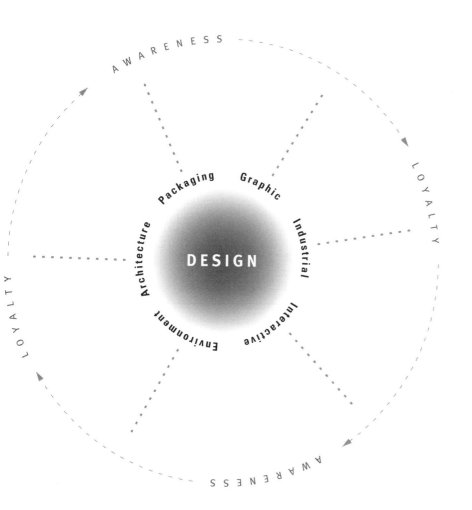

A brand identity that is distinctive and differentiated from its competitors will always help a client legally protect this valuable and critical asset. Almost anything that serves to distinguish products or services from those of a competitor can serve as a trademark. Names, symbols, logotypes, taglines, slogans, packaging and product design, color, and sound are all brand identity assets that can be registered with the federal government and protected from future litigation.

Federal registration is in place to ensure that the consumer is not confused or misled by trademarks that are too similar. The government agency responsible is called the U.S. Patent and Trademark Office (USPTO). Trademarks are always registered within industry classes, of which there are forty-five, and may be registered in more than one class. Intellectual property is the name of the legal discipline that specializes in providing the broadest scope of protection for brand identity assets. Intellectual property assets also include copyrights and patents.

There are different points in the brand identity process when research is conducted to determine whether there are any conflicting marks, names, or taglines. The various types of searches include common-law, federal, and state. Experienced legal counsel is needed to assess the risk of trademark infringement.

A distinctive identity is worth nothing unless you can protect it.

Roberta Jacobs-Meadway, Ballard Spahr Andrews & Ingersoll

The brand identity legal process

Establish legal needs	*Establish legal resources*	*Decide type of search*
Determine what needs to be protected: name, symbol, logotype, packaging, product design	Identify client legal counsel	Common-law (anyone can conduct)
Determine type of registration: federal, state, country	Identify intellectual property lawyer	Short screening (level 1)
Identify key dates	Review other proprietary assets	Comprehensive
Identify any regulatory constraints	Research search services	Visual (for symbols, package, products)
Determine industry class(es)		
Establish search responsibilities		
Set up documentation system		

Brand identity legal basics

1 The more differentiated an identity is from its competitors, the easier it is to protect from a legal perspective.

2 Registering a mark gives clients extra rights and the broadest scope of protection. Although trademark rights may be established by actual use, federal registration ultimately secures more benefits in trademark infringement.

3 Registration is at the federal and state level. State registrations are usually less expensive than federal registrations but are more subject to challenge.

4 Protection for marks in other countries must be sought country by country, since legal protection differs from country to country.

5 An individual, a corporation, a joint venture, or a partnership can own a trademark. A trademark cannot have two independent owners.

6 In the case of litigation, if the defendant failed to do a competent search, it may be evidence of bad faith.

7 Intellectual property is a specialty, and identifying a lawyer who has experience in this is critical. Anyone can search the USPTO or other databases on the web for federal registrations, but lawyers are trained to assess the risk of a brand identity strategy.

8 Certain industries, such as the financial industry, require state registrations with designated commissioners for product names that are sold nationally. What works in one state will not necessarily work in another.

9 Mergers usually have their own set of requirements that affect information sharing. Parties may request to restrict access to certain documents.

What do those little marks mean?

® may only be used when marks have been federally registered.

™ is used to alert the public, and does not require filing federal applications. It means trademark, which is a claim of ownership for goods and packaging.

SM means service mark, and refers to a unique service. It appears on any form of advertising and promotional literature. It does not require filing federal registration.

Myths

Once you register it, you own it forever and for everything.

Registering a domain name offers legal protection.

We can save money if we do it ourselves.

By the end of 2001, the USPTO had 1,063,164 active registrations for trademarks.

Conduct preliminary research

- Determine quickly other ownership
- Search domain registration sites, newspapers, search engines, telephone directories
- Create short list for comprehensive search

Conduct comprehensive research

- Identity comprehensive database resources for naming, symbols, taglines, trade dress (package design), product design, color, sound
- Conduct and review searches
- Determine availability
- Choose what to eliminate or contest

Conduct registration

- Finalize list of registrations
- Create documents as required
- Federal
- State
- Country

Monitor and educate

- Develop plan to monitor intellectual property assets
- Conduct annual intellectual property audits
- Educate employees and vendors
- Publish standards that clarify proper usage
- Make it easy to adhere to legal usage

The art of correspondence and the letterhead have lasted from the quill pen through the typewriter and the computer. Although voice mails and e-mails have become the most widely used form of communication, the letterhead is not yet obsolete in the beginning of the twenty-first century. The letter still comes to us in the same way that it has been coming to us since Ben Franklin became the first U.S. postmaster—unless, of course, it comes via FedEx.

The letterhead, offset-printed on fine paper, remains a core application in the brand identity system even though some companies have begun to send out electronic letterheads as attachments. The letterhead with an original signature is still an important conduit for doing business. It is regarded as a credible proof of being in business, and frequently carries an important message or contractual agreement. It is still regarded as the most formal type of business communication, and has an implicit dignity. For many years, banks required businesses to write a letter on their letterhead in order to open an account.

In America, the standard letterhead size is 8½" by 11". This size is referred to as the U.S. standard size, and is also used in Canada and Mexico. The rest of the world, however, uses letterhead and envelopes based on the metric system.

Characters:
Summerford Design

The letterhead design process

Clarify use	*Determine need*	*Get content*
Letters, short and long	Corporate only	Best-case scenario
Contracts	Division letterhead	Worst-case scenario
Memos	Personal letterhead	Unify abbreviations
Invoices	Size	Tagline
		Regulatory info
		Parent
		Professional affiliation

Letterhead design basics

1 Never design a letterhead without an actual letter on the page.

2 Take into consideration the location of the folds.

3 Get an ink draw on the paper that you have chosen.

4 Do a fax test.

5 Design a second sheet.

6 Research the right size for a foreign country.

7 Feel the paper and identify the proper weight.

8 Find out biases regarding formats.

9 Provide guidelines for letter positioning.

10 Always test the paper and envelopes on a laser printer.

The world of abbreviations

There are no universal abbreviations. Consistency is the rule.

Telephone

Phone
Tel
P
T
Voice
V
☎

Facsimile

Fax
F

Mobile

Cellular
M

E-mail

e-mail
e
(just address)

Website

Web
(just domain)

Home

Home

Characters' extensive paper application system builds on its core identity. Characters provides computer generated production services.

Develop design

– Use real letter
– Show actual size
– Examine iterations
– Design envelopes

Identify paper

– Appropriate surface
– Availability
– Laser compatibility
– Color

Determine production method

– Printing
– Engraving
– Foil stamping
– Embossing
– Watermark

Manage production

– Review proofs
– Watch first run on press
– Develop electronic templates

Each day, millions of people all over the world are asking others, "May I have your card?" This commonplace business ritual looks different around the globe. In Korea, one shows respect for a colleague by presenting a business card in two hands. In the Far East, most corporate business cards are two-sided, with one side, for example, in Korean, and the other side in English. The Western-size business card is slowly becoming the standard around the world, although many countries are still using variations of a larger card.

In the nineteenth century, Victorian calling cards were elaborately decorated and oversized by present American standards. They were designed to showcase a name only. Today, the designer is faced with so much information to include—from e-mail to voice mail to mobile phone and 800 numbers, double addresses and domains—that the small business card is a challenge even for the most experienced designers. Information, by necessity, is flowing to the back side.

The business card is a small and portable marketing tool. The quality and intelligence of the information are a reflection on the card holder and her company. Digital business cards are gaining in popularity—these mini CDs have the capacity to hold a multimedia presentation on the size of a credit card. In the future, a high-tech business card may double as an identification card, and include a user's fingerprint or other biometric data.

Like the best packages, the best calling cards convey trustworthiness and WOW at once.

Tom Peters, author, Brand You

The business card design process

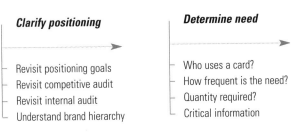

Clarify positioning

- Revisit positioning goals
- Revisit competitive audit
- Revisit internal audit
- Understand brand hierarchy

Determine need

- Who uses a card?
- How frequent is the need?
- Quantity required?
- Critical information

Finalize content

- Best-case scenario
- Worst-case scenario
- Unify abbreviations
- Tagline
- Regulatory info
- Parent
- Professional affiliation

Business card design basics

1 Think of a business card as a marketing tool.

2 Make it easy for the receiver of a card to retrieve information.

3 Make it easy for new cards to be produced.

4 Minimize the amount of information, within reason.

5 Consider using the back as a place for more information or a marketing message.

6 Carefully choose the weight of the paper to convey quality.

7 Feel the paper and the surface.

8 Make sure all abbreviations are consistent.

9 Make sure that the titles are consistent.

10 Make sure that the typographic use of caps and lower case is consistent.

11 Develop system formats.

12 Don't consider an unusual size unless the company is a restaurant or fashion house.

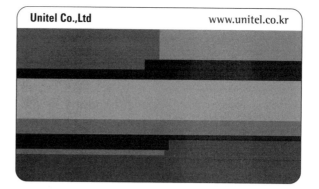

Unitel Co.,Ltd   www.unitel.co.kr

유니텔 주식회사
서울특별시 서초구 서초동 1449-6번지 한원빌딩, 137-070
4th Fl, Hanwon Bldg., 1449-6, Seocho-dong, Seocho-gu, Seoul, Korea
Tel : 02-3415-6948 Fax: 02-3415-6101
e-mail : chulsoo@unitel.co.kr

김 철 수 Chulsoo Kim
책임/전략기획 Planning Manager
마케팅팀 Marketing Team

UNITEL

Infinite, a strategic identity and image management firm in Seoul, Korea designed these bilingual, two-sided business cards for Daehan Investment Trust Securities and Unitel, an internet provider.

150-705 서울특별시 영등포구 여의도동 27-3번지
Tel : 02-3771-7091 Fax : 02-782-8606 H.P : 011-3283-0154
E-mail : chulsoo@daetoo.com www.daetoo.com

김 철 수 홍보실/차장

 대한투자 신탁 증권

...ong, Youngdungpo-Ku, Seoul 150-705, Korea
...1-7091 Fax : 82-2-782-8606 H.P : 011-3283-0154
...oo@daetoo.com www.daetoo.com

Chulsoo Kim Planning Manager/Marketing Team

Develop design	*Identify paper*	*Determine production method*	*Manage production*
Use real text	Appropriate surface	Printing	Review proofs
Show actual size	Weight	Engraving	Watch first run on press
Examine iterations	Availability	Foil stamping	
Consider the back	Color	Embossing	
Develop color strategy	Quality		

You're waiting for your café latte and see brochures in a stylish rack. You rip open your monthly mutual fund statement and there it is—an insert. You unpack your new iPod and there's a tiny booklet. You go to the doctor and each aspect of your health care has its own publication. You contact a consultant and he encourages you to download his company's brochure. Brochures are omnipresesnt.

Brochures continue to be popular marketing and information tools. The best brochures invite readership since they're easy to understand and user friendly. Designing a unified system ensures that the identity of the company is consistently presented and communicates familiarity to the existing customer. Designing a grid and typographic system that allows flexibility is not only smart from a branding perspective, but also efficient from a cost and resources perspective.

Empire Blue Cross & Blue Shield:
Bernhardt Fudyma Design Group

The brochure system design process

Revisit the big picture

- Examine positioning goals
- Examine competitive audit
- Examine internal audit
- Identify functional needs, i.e., how brochures are used and distributed
- Understand how brochures are produced within the company
- Identify challenges

Design a cover system

- Examine signature scenarios:
  Signature in primary and constant place
  Split signature
  Signature not used on cover
  Signature used on back only
  Signature used in secondary position with product name in primary position

Determine typographic system

- One typeface family or many
- Title typeface
- Cover descriptor typeface
- Header typeface
- Subhead typeface
- Text typeface
- Caption typeface

Determine artwork

- Photography
- Illustration
- Collage
- Typographic
- Abstract
- Identity derivative

Brochure system basics

1 Unified brochure systems increase brand recognition.

2 Effective brochure systems are differentiated from the competition's.

3 Brochures are an extension of a company's identity and brand architecture.

4 Effective brochures make it easy for a customer to understand information and to buy products and services.

5 By making information accessible, a company demonstrates its understanding of its customers' needs and preferences.

6 Effective brochures make it easier for the sales force to sell.

7 Effective systems anticipate future change.

8 System standards should be easy to understand by managers, design professionals, and advertising agencies.

9 Systems should include flexible elements but not waver on clear, absolute standards regarding signatures.

10 Great design is effective only if it can be reproduced at the highest quality.

11 The best brochures are well written and present appropriate amounts of information.

12 Systems should include a consistent call for action that gives the customer choices and access.

Bernhardt Fudyma Design Group created a flexible graphic system for Empire Blue Cross & Blue Shield that unified all marketing and communication materials and positioned their client as New York State's leading provider of health insurance.

Design color family	**Choose standard formats**	**Choose paper**	**Develop prototypes**	**Develop guidelines**
– Two-color	– 4 × 9	– Examine functionality	– Use real copy	– Articulate goals
– Four-color	– 6 × 9	– Examine price points	– Look at best- and worst-case scenarios	– Create grids
– Flat colors	– 8.5 × 11	– Decide on family of papers	– Edit language as needed	– Explain system
– Web colors	– Other	– Have dummies made	– Demonstrate flexibility of system	– Develop templates
		– Feel the paper	– Decide on signature configurations	– Monitor execution
		– Consider weight if needed		

The best packages become one with our brand experience. Packages are brands that you trust enough to take into your home. For baby boomers, they reside forever in their childhood memories—from the Whitman sampler box and the Beatles *White Album* cover to the glass Coca-Cola bottle and the Tiffany box. For Generation X, packages themselves have evolved into status symbols. The lexicon of cool includes the Absolut vodka bottle, the wavy and futuristic Gatorade bottle, the Abercrombie & Fitch paper bag, and the Tiffany box.

Regardless of our age, we are continually comforted and cajoled by packaging shapes, graphics, colors, messages, and containers. The shelf is probably the most competitive marketing environment that exists. From new brands to extending or revitalizing existing product lines, considerations of brand equity, cost, time, and competition are often complex.

Packaging design is a specialty, and routinely involves collaboration with industrial designers, packaging engineers, and manufacturers. In the food and pharmaceutical industry, it is regulated by the government. Package design is only one part of the puzzle involved in a product launch. Timetables include packaging approval and production, sales force meetings, product sell into stores, manufacturing and distribution, and advertising.

In the average half-hour trip to the supermarket, 30,000 products vie for the shopper's attention.

Thomas Hine, author, The Total Package

The packaging development process

Clarify goals + positioning	*Conduct audits + Identify expert team*	*Conduct research as needed*	*Research legal requirements*	*Research functional criteria*
Establish goals and define the problem	Competitive (category)	Understand brand equity	Brand + corporate standards:	Product stability
Brand equity	Retail (point of sale)	Determine brand standards	Product-specific	Tamper or theft resistance
Competition	Brand (internal, existing product line)	Examine brand architecture	Net weight	Shelf footprint
Existing brands in product line	Packaging designer	Clarify target consumer	Drug Facts	Durability
Price point	Packaging engineer	Confirm need for product—does product benefit resonate?	Nutrition Facts	Usage
Target consumer	Packaging manufacturers	Confirm language—how should benefit be expressed?	Ingredients	Packability
Product benefit	Industrial designers		Warnings	Fillability
	Regulatory legal department		Claims	

Packaging Basics

1 The shelf is the most competitive marketing environment that exists.

2 Good design sells. It is a competitive advantage.

3 Positioning relative to the competition and to the other members of the product line is critical for developing a packaging strategy.

4 A disciplined, coherent approach leads to a unified, powerful brand presence.

5 Structure and graphics can be developed concurrently. It's a chicken-and-egg debate.

6 When designing a brand extension, there is always a strategic tug-of-war between differentiation and coherence within a product line.

7 Consider the entire life cycle of the package and its relationship to the product: source, print, assemble, pack, preserve, ship, display, purchase, use, recycle/dispose.

8 Timetables involving packaging approval and production, sales force meetings, product sell in to stores, manufacturing and distribution.

9 Developing a new structure takes a long time and is very expensive but it offers a unique competitive advantage.

It's no longer enough to just research the competition. One needs to think beyond the category when designing a new structure. We live at a time when one buys tuna in a bag, bath salts in a paint can, and wine in a carton.

Steve Perry, Bailey Design Group

Johnson & Johnson Clean and Clear: Bailey Design Group

With minimum sales help in a retail environment, a package must be a silent salesperson.

Russ Napolitano, Bailey Design Group

Zours: Bailey Design Group

First I bought it because it looked cool. Later I bought it because it tasted good.

Michael Grillo, age 14

Determine printing specs	**Determine structural design**	**Finalize copy**	**Design and prototype**	**Evaluate solution + manage production**
Method: Flexo, litho, roto	Design new structure or use stock?	Product name	Start with face panels (2D renderings)	In a retail/competitive environment
Application: direct, label, shrink-wrap label	Choose forms (i.e., carton, bottle, can, tube, jar, tin, blister packs)	Benefit copy	Get prototypes made	As a member of the product line
Other: number of colors, divinyl, UPC code, minimums for knockouts, etc.	Choose possible materials, substrates, or finishes	Ingredients	Narrow option(s)	Consumer testing
	Source stock and get samples	Nutrition Facts/Drug Facts	Design rest of package	Finalize files
		Net contents	Simulate reality: use actual structure/substrate with contents	Oversee production
		Claims		
		Warnings		
		Distributed by		
		Manufactured in		
		UPC code		

More then any other application, a website simulates the brand personality of a company. Its palette of engaging content, sound, movement, and color creates a walking, talking interactive company experience. It's the next best thing to reality, and in some cases it's more efficient, more user-friendly, and faster. The customer is in charge. Aside from access to meaningful information, the Internet provides the customer with a no-pressure sales environment, and at the click of a mouse, a competitor is waiting.

The best websites understand their customers and respect their needs and preferences. A company's website should quickly answer these questions: "Who is this company? Why does anyone need to know? What's in it for me?" Expressing an authentic brand identity on the web is still a new frontier that communication architects and information architects, designers and engineers are just beginning to conquer. Websites are increasingly used as portals for media tools. From images to logos and message points, downloading from a site allows employees to jump-start marketing and communications from anywhere in the field or around the world.

Cybermedia require nonlinear thinking, inviting interfaces, and creative intelligence.

Stella Gassaway, Stellarvisions

Intranets like QVC's customer service tool must express the culture and the aspirations of the enterprise.

Stella Gassaway

Website development process

Compiled by Stellarvisions

Initiate plan	*Build groundwork*	*Define structure*	*Prepare content*
Set goals	Conduct competitive audit	Outline content	Set editorial calendar
Establish project team	Gather data about audience	Map content	Decide how often content change
Identify audiences	Consider content sources	Define logical relationships	Identify existing content
Define key messages	Explore technological issues	Create user scenarios	Rewrite text for web
Revisit positioning	Evaluate existing site	Build wire-frame prototypes	Commission new content, visual media assets
Set priorities	Revisit goals + set strategies	Test prototypes	Approve content including legal signoff
Rough out project plan			Review content in screen context
Define success			Edit and proofread text

Website basics

1. Keep site goals, audience needs, key messages, and brand personality central to every decision about the site.

2. Anticipate future change and growth.

3. Site structure should not simply reflect organizational structure.

4. Begin site structure with content, not a screen design.

5. Do not force content into counterintuitive groupings.

6. Write content specifically for the web.

7. Conduct usability testing.

8. Observe etiquette. Alert visitors where special technology is needed, where a screen may load slowly, or where a link leaves your site.

9. Comply with ADA—arrange for visually impaired visitors to use software to read the site aloud or greatly magnify text.

10. At each stage ask: Is the message clear? Is the content accessible? Is the experience positive?

11. Confront internal political agendas that may sabatoge site goals.

Characteristics of the best websites

Easy to use/learn

Meet visitor expectations

Communicate visually

According to Panoptic Communications, the number one Internet myth is "Build it and they will come."

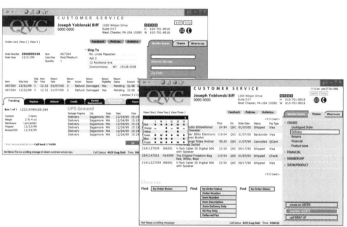

QVC: Stellarvisions

Create visual design	*Develop technical design*	*Finalize development*	*Launch and maintain*
Color palette, tone, metaphor	Strategy for data integration	Production of screen graphics	Promote site launch
Grid and element placement	Static vs. dynamic screens	Development of HTML templates	Complete style guide
Graphic elements + text styles	Transaction flow design	Content freeze	Optimize site for search engines
Navigational cues	Quality assurance testing plan	Insert content into screens	Develop maintenance plan
Layouts of key screens	Security + scalability	Approval of beta site	Monitor logs and user paths
Interface for functions	Technical specifications	Test beta site for quality	Measure success
Integration of media	Prototype and test	User tests of beta site	Ongoing usability testing
Prototype and test with users	Lock feature set		

Communication in the environment provides yet another opportunity to build a brand. From city streets and skylines through museums and airports, signage functions as identification, information, and advertising. There is substantial evidence that effective retail signage increases revenues, and intelligent wayfinding systems support and enhance the experience of a brand, whether it's a town, a university, or a business district.

Signage design as a discipline has come a long way since the hand-painted Burma Shave highway advertising signs of the fifties. City skylines have become illuminated with brand identification. Signage systems around the world are playing an increasing role in expressing and revitalizing the image and experience of a destination. In Seoul, Korea, large digital billboards grace the sides of skyscrapers to capture our attention. Digital media open the door for interactive storytelling.

In the eighteenth century, laws required innkeepers to have their signs high enough to clear an armored man on horseback. In the twenty-first century, cities and towns around the world routinely revise sign codes in order to create environments that support the image that a community wants to portray, and to regulate standards to protect public safety.

Signage helps people identify, navigate, and understand environments.

Alan Jacobson, principal, AGS

Signage design process

Establish goals

- Determine project scope
- Understand audience needs + habits
- Clarify positioning
- Clarify function
- Develop time frame + budget

Build project team

- Client facilities manager
- Information design firm
- Fabricator
- Architect or space designer
- Lighting consultant

Conduct research

- Site audit: environment
- Site audit: building type
- User habits and patterns
- Local codes and zoning
- Consideration for the disabled
- Weather + traffic conditions
- Materials and finishes
- Fabrication processes

Establish project criteria

- Legibility
- Placement
- Visibility
- Sustainability
- Safety
- Maintenance
- Security
- Modularity

Solow Building Company: Chermayeff & Geismar

On West 57th Street in New York sits a fat, bright red, giant "9." I love it. (It) is probably the only trademark that not only doubles as a street number but also developed into a meeting point, a landmark.

Stefan Sagmeister, designer

Signage basics

1 Signage expresses the brand, and builds on understanding the needs and habits of users in the environment.

2 Legibility, visibility, durability, and positioning must drive the design process. Distance, speed, light, color, and contrast affect legibility.

3 Signage is a mass communications medium that works 24/7 and can attract new customers, influence purchasing decisions, and increase sales.

4 Exterior signage must take into consideration both vehicular and pedestrian traffic.

5 Every community, industrial park, and shopping mall develops its own signage code; there are no universal codes.

6 Signage codes affect material, illumination (electrical), and structural choices; zoning or land use issues affect placement and size of signage.

7 Zoning constraints need to be understood prior to design development.

8 Permit and variance applications should include the benefit to the land use planning scheme.

9 Signage requires a long-term commitment, and maintenance plans and contracts are critical to protecting the investment.

10 Developing prototypes minimize risk by testing design prior to fabrication.

11 Signage should always complement the overall architecture and land use of a site.

12 Signage standards manuals include various configurations, materials, supplier selections, and production, installation, and maintenance details.

Schematic design	*Design development*	*Documentation*	*Fabrication + Maintenance*
– Brand identity system	– Begin variance process	– Complete working drawings	– Check shop drawings
– Color, scale, format	– Prepare prototypes or models	– Construction, mounting, and elevation details	– Inspect work
– Typography	– Finalize content	– Final specifications	– Manage fabrication
– Lighting	– Create drawings or renderings	– Placement plans	– Manage installation
– Materials and finishes	– Choose materials + color samples	– Bid documents	– Develop maintenance plan
– Fabrication techniques		– Permit applications	
– Mounting + hardware			
– Placement			

From a luxury car showroom to the inside of an airplane or a supermarket, smart businesses seize every opportunity to manage the experience and expectations of the customer by branding the environment. Fabergé, the goldsmith known for the splendid jeweled eggs for the czar, was one of the first global entrepreneurs to understand that a well-conceived showroom appeals to customers and increases sales. We live at a time when it's not unusual for the design and ambience of a restaurant to be a greater attraction than the culinary art, or for a financial services company, such as ING Direct, to open a hip café to serve up good coffee and financial advice.

The exterior architecture represents yet another opportunity to stimulate immediate recognition and attract customers. In the nineteen fifties, an orange tile roof in the distance sent an immediate and welcoming signal that there was a Howard Johnson's restaurant ahead. At the opposite end of the cultural spectrum, the architecture of the Guggenheim Museum at Bilbao *is* the brand and a powerful magnet that draws millions of visitors.

Architects and space designers, graphic designers, industrial designers, lighting experts, structural and mechanical engineers, general contractors and subcontractors, and a host of manufacturer's reps collaborate with client development teams to create unique environments and experiences that make their clients more successful. Memorable and unique color, texture, scale, light, sound, movement, comfort, smell, and accessible information are strategies used to manage perception in the environment.

Milton Glaser created a team of architects, graphic and industrial designers to reinvent the modern supermarket for Grand Union, a chain of more than five hundred stores. By challenging assumptions about how to present food and inform the customer, the unifying principle was "Make it easy to find everything. Customers will like the experience and will come back more often." Over a twenty-year period, Glaser developed new information systems, changed the aisle system, varied the quality of light, and redesigned packaging for over a thousand products.

A dramatic facade of waterproof photographic panels attracted customers and was achievable within a modest budget.

Branded environment imperatives

1 Understand the needs, preferences, habits, and aspirations of the target audience.

2 Create a unique experience that is aligned with brand positioning.

3 Experience and study the competition and learn from their successes and failures.

4 Create an experience and environment that make it easy for customers to buy, and that inspire them to come back again and again.

5 Align the quality and speed of service with the experience of the environment.

6 Create an environment that helps the sales force sell and makes it easy to complete a transaction.

7 Consider the dimensions of space: visual, auditory, olfactory, tactile, and thermal.

8 Understand the psychological effect of light and lighting sources, and consider energy efficiency whenever possible.

9 Consider all operational needs so that the client can deliver on the brand promise.

10 Understand traffic flow, the volume of business, and economic considerations.

11 Align merchandising strategies with displays, advertising, and sales strategies.

12 Design a space that is sustainable, durable, and easy to maintain and clean.

13 Consider the needs of handicapped customers.

We're starved for Wow! For experiences that coddle, comfort, cajole, and generally show us a darn good time. That's what we want for the money. I want decent vittles, mind you, but food we can get anywhere.

Hilary Jay, design critic

Gucci has redesigned their retail experience. It's not a radical jump—it has to do with who they are, and it builds on their history with a new eye to the future—and a streamlined presence.

Trish Thompson, fashion consultant

*Wherever I may wander
Whenever I may roam
When I walk into a Starbucks
I'm suddenly back at home.*

Cathy Jooste, global citizen

Grand Union: Milton Glaser

Building brand awareness on the road is easier than ever. Once the exclusive domain of sign painters, vehicles now represent a new large moving canvas where almost any type of communication is possible. Whether on an urban thruway at rush hour or a remote country road at sunset, the goal remains the same—make the brand identity immediately recognizable and do it within a few seconds.

From trains to planes to large vans and small delivery trucks, vehicles are omnipresent. Vehicle graphics are experienced from ground level, from other vehicles such as cars and buses, and from the windows of buildings. Designers need to consider scale, legibility, distance, surface color, and the effects of movement, speed, and light. They also need to consider the life of the vehicle, the durability of the signage medium, and safety requirements and regulations that may vary state by state.

The Goodyear blimp and the hot-air balloon are early examples of brand identities taking flight. There is nothing more beautiful than the sleek design of jets on the runway displaying their distinctive identities. Many vehicles carry other messages— from taglines and phone numbers to graphic elements and vehicle identification numbers.

JoongAng Ilbo, Korea: Infinite

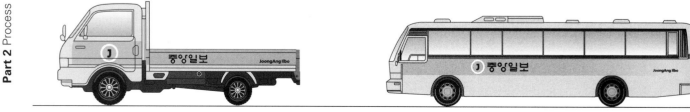

Vehicle signage process

Plan	*Design*	*Determine*	*Examine*	*Implement*
Audit vehicle types	Choose base color for vehicle	Fabrication methods: Decal and wrap	Impact on insurance rates	Files done to spec
Revisit positioning	Design placement of signature	Vinyl	Life of vehicle	Documentation for installer
Research fabrication methods	Determine other messages:	Magnetic	Life of sign type	Examine output
Research installers	Phone number or domain	Hand-painted	Cost and time	Test colors
Receive technical specifications	Vehicle ID number		Safety or other regulations	Manage installation
Get vehicle drawings	Tagline			
	Explore other graphic elements			

Vehicle types

Public

Buses

Trains

Ferries

Private

Container trucks

Delivery trucks

Helicopters

Planes

Motorcycles

Jitneys

Hot-air balloons

Blimps

Daejeon University, Korea: Infinite

Chohung Bank, Korea: Infinite

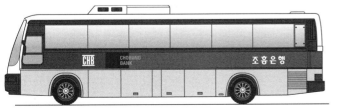

Halla Winia Ice Hockey Club: Infinite   113

Clothing communicates. From the friendly orange apron at Home Depot to a UPS delivery person needing a signature, a visible and distinctive uniform simplifies customer transactions. A uniform can also signal authority and identification. From the airline captain to the security guard, uniforms make customers more at ease. Finding a waiter in a restaurant may be as simple as finding the person with the black T-shirt and the white pants. On the playing field, teams require uniforms that will not only distinguish them from their competitors but also look good on television. A lab coat is a required uniform in a laboratory, as are scrubs in an O.R., and are subject to regulations and compliance standards.

The best uniforms engender pride and are appropriate to the workplace and environment. Their designers are respectful of the individuals who need to wear them, and carefully consider performance criteria such as durability and mobility. The way an employee is dressed affects the way that the individual and her organization are perceived. The reproduction method, placement, and scale of the signature are critical decisions that build awareness.

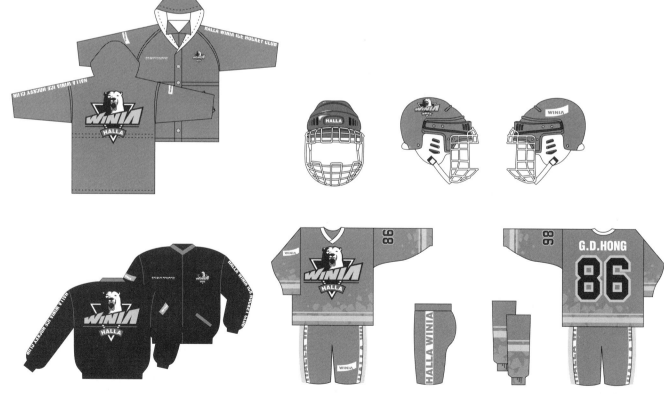

Halla Winia Ice Hockey Club, Korea:
Infinite

Uniform performance criteria

Functional: does the uniform take into consideration the nature of the job?

Durability: is the uniform well made?

Ease: is the uniform machine washable or easy to clean?

Mobility: can employees do their tasks easily?

Comfort: is the uniform comfortable?

Visibility: is the uniform immediately recognizable?

Wearability: is the uniform easy to put on?

Weight: has the weight been considered?

Temperature: does the uniform consider weather factors?

Pride: does the uniform engender pride?

Respect: does the uniform respect different body sizes?

Safety: does the uniform adhere to regulations?

Brand: is the uniform a reflection of the desired image?

Uniform possibilities

Aprons

Belts

Pants

Shorts

Skirts

Turtlenecks

Golf shirt

T-shirt

Vests

Neckwear

Outerwear

Rainwear

Blazers

Blouses

Bows

Gloves

Boots

Helmets

Shoes

Socks

Tights

ID badges

Accessories

Scarves

Fleece

Windwear

Visors

Baseball caps

Scrub apparel

Patient gowns

Lab coats

Who needs uniforms?

Public safety

Security

Transportation

Couriers

Bank tellers

Volunteers

Health care

Hospitality

Retail

Restaurants

Sports teams

Sports facilities

Laboratories

Special events

Entertainment

Universities

Schools

Methods

Off the shelf

Custom design

Custom fabrication

Embroidery

Screen printing

Patches

Striping

A trade show is not a trade show without giveaways. The best booths also give you canvas bags to store all your goodies, from squeezy stress balls to commuter cups, baseball caps, and mouse pads. One wonders how one ever lived without this memorabilia.

Ephemera is defined as objects with a short life, or more simply put, stuff. Companies frequently use stuff that carries their brand identity as marketing and promotion items. Done right, these tchotchkes build brand awareness and are good public relations and thank-you's. Many large companies have company stores on their website so that employees can be completely outfitted in any weather condition. The best clothing that carries an identity is tastefully designed and produced with quality. A nice polo can engender pride, and it can also be a nice client gift.

Reproduction is never as simple as a vendor might think. Special techniques such as embroidery onto a golf shirt or leather stamping onto a portfolio usually require a custom signature that understands the needs of the production technique. The best way to control quality is to examine a proof.

American Folk Art Museum:
Pentagram

The Possibilities

Pens

Pencils

Highlighters

Mugs

Commuter cups

Steins

Coasters

Apothecary jars

Sports bottles

Portfolios

Pad holders

CD cases

Folders

Pocket planners

Letter openers

Mouse pads

Screen sweeps

Notepads

Memo cubes

3M Post-its

Magnets

Rulers

Balloons

Tins

Yo-yos

Frisbees

Playing cards

Stress balls

Beach balls

Wooden nickels

Hand flyers

Lanyards

Neck wallets

Key chains

Tools

Flashlights

X-strobes

Clocks

Watches

Globes

Calculators

Calendars

Totes

Luggage tags

Sports duffels

Golf balls

Golf tees

Golf umbrellas

Visors

Lapel pins

T-shirts

Golf shirts

Denim shirts

Sweatshirts

Parkas

Rain jackets

Throws

American Folk Art Museum:
Pentagram

Managing brand identity assets requires enlightened leadership and a long-term commitment to doing everything possible to build the brand. The mandate to build the brand must come from the top. If management's commitment is tepid and the resources committed are minimal, the original investment will most likely deliver a dismal rate of return.

To the surprise of many clients, the brand identity process does not end after corporate letterhead and business cards are printed. This is when the work really begins. Because it takes quite a while to get to this point of visible accomplishment, many managers assume that the time, money, and energy spent thus far represent the majority of the investment. Wrong. It's just the beginning. Creating the brand identity was the easy part. Managing these assets well is harder.

The first step in managing brand assets is deployment. There are three key initiatives that require careful attention. Communicating with employees about the new brand identity is the first initiative and highest priority. This is also called the internal launch. The second initiative is the creation of standards and guidelines to ensure that all future applications will adhere to the original vision and intention of the program. The third initiative is to launch the new brand identity externally to key stakeholders.

Two other priorities include creating accountability—identifying those people who champion the brand, developing a checks-and-balances method to audit progress.

The brand is a living animate object. As a result, you need to constantly monitor it and make certain that it continues to be differentiated and relevant to its constituencies.

Clay Timon, CEO, Landor Associates

JoongAng Ilbo is one of the leading daily newspapers from Korea. Their brand identity, designed by Infinite, features the letter "J" in the shape of an ear in the middle of a circle. The tagline, "We will be the eyes and ears of the public" is reinforced by the circle which stands for the earth. The identity places JoongAng Ilbo at the center of the world. Their standards are extensive, and anticipate every category of applications.

Rare is the person in an organization who embraces change. Introducing a new name and identity to an existing organization or to merged entities is exponentially more difficult than creating a brand for a new company. Changing brand identity means that whatever was on a manager's plate now doubles. The to-do list is extremely long, even in a small company. New brand identity implementation requires a vigilant strategic focus, advance planning, obsession with detail, and some acid indigestion pills or whatever helps you to just put your head down and do it.

Routinely, the director of marketing and public relations will oversee the change. In larger organizations, an individual may be retained to focus exclusively on implementation. The skills required are knowledge of branding, public relations, communications, identity design, production, and organizational management. Military mobilization skills come in handy, and some boundless optimism doesn't hurt either.

Managing brand identity change has the potential to enhance brand perception—by increasing awareness among constituencies, increasing preference for an institution, and building loyalty.

Patricia M. Baldridge, VP, marketing and public relations, Philadelphia University

New brand identity affects

Stationery, business cards, forms

Faxes, e-mail signatures

Signage

Advertising

Website

Marketing materials

Uniforms and name tags

Customers, vendors, contractors

Directory listings

Voice mail, phone answering

Biggest challenges of brand identity change

Developed by Patricia M. Baldridge

1 Time and money: planning enough advance time and an adequate budget

2 Deciding whether to go for a mega-launch or a phased-in launch

3 Internal buy-in and support

4 Keeping a strategic focus on all communications

5 Helping people to make the connection from old to new

6 Honoring one's heritage while celebrating the new

7 Identifying the broadest list of stakeholders affected by the change

8 Helping people who have trouble with the change through a transition

9 Effectively communicating the essence of the brand within time and money constraints

10 Creating and maintaining message consistency

11 Reaching all audiences

12 Building excitement and understanding

Key beliefs

A strategic focus centers on the brand.

Brand identity can help to center a company on its mission.

A mega-launch means less chance for confusion and complications.

Clarity about key messages surrounding launch is critical.

Go internal first before you go external.

Once is never enough to communicate a new idea.

You need to sell a new name and build meaning.

Different audiences may require different messages.

Do whatever you can to keep the momentum going.

Recognize that an identity program is more than a new name or new logo.

Name change essentials

1 A sound reason for changing the name is the first and most critical step.

2 The change must have the potential to enhance the company's public perception, recognition, recruitment, customer relations, partnerships, etc.

3 Accept the fact that there will be resistance.

4 Keep the momentum going by creating an air of excitement.

5 Targeted messages are better but cost more.

Get ready. Get set. Launch. A launch represents a huge marketing opportunity to communicate with customers and other stakeholders about the brand. Smart organizations seize this opportunity to build brand awareness and synergy, and to communicate that they are on the move. Different circumstances demand different launch strategies—from multimedia campaigns, company-wide meetings, and road tours to a T-shirt for each employee. Some organizations execute massive visible change, including external signage and vehicles, virtually overnight, while others choose a phased approach.

Clearly small organizations don't have the budget or the need for a multimedia campaign. Smart organizations create a sales call opportunity to present a new card, or send a PDF announcement to each customer, colleague, and vendor. Others use existing marketing channels, such as inserting a brochure with the monthly statement.

In nearly every launch, the most important audience is a company's employees because it gives an organization an opportunity to help employees reconnect with their company's vision, what the brand stands for, and its core values. Regardless of the scope and budget, a launch requires a comprehensive communications plan. Rarely is the best launch strategy no strategy, which is the business-as-usual or un-launch. On occasion, an organization may not want to draw attention from the financial community or its shareholders, so it may choose to do nothing.

Key pre-launch questions

Who needs to know?

What do they need to know?

Why do they need to know?

Does the change affect them?

How are they going to find out?

When are they going to find out?

Launch strategic goals

1 Increase brand awareness and understanding among all stakeholders, including the general public

2 Increase preference for the company and its programs and services

3 Build loyalty for the company

4 Promote the new identity as a brand

5 Create an emotional connection with stakeholders

6 Positively influence your constituents' choices and/or behavior

Comprehensive plan includes

Goals and objectives of the new brand identity

Communications activities around brand implementation

Timeline for implementation and budget

How identity is aligned with company goals

How identity is aligned with research

The company's target audiences

The company's major messages

Communications strategies (including internal communications, public relations, advertising, and direct marketing)

Internal training strategy for employees

Standards and guidelines strategy

Methods

Organization-wide meetings

Press releases

Special events

Q & A hotline on website

Script of consistent messages

Print, radio, TV ads

Trade publications

Direct mail

Launch website

External launch basics

Timing is everything. Find the window.

Create consistent messages.

Target messages.

Create the right media mix.

Leverage public relations, marketing, and customer service.

Make sure your sales force knows the launch strategy.

Be customer-focused.

Schedule a lot of advance time.

Seize every opportunity to garner marketing synergy.

Tell them, tell them again, and then tell them again.

Internal launch basics

Make a moment. Create a buzz.

Communicate why this is important.

Tell them why you did it.

Communicate what it means.

Talk about future goals and mission.

Review identity basics: meaning, sustainability.

Convey that this is a top-down initiative.

Make employees brand champions and ambassadors.

Show concrete examples of how employees can live the brand.

Give employees a sense of ownership.

Give them something tangible: a card, a T-shirt.

Since the electronic and brand revolution, standards have become much more accessible, dynamic, and easy to produce. From a website to a CD to a fact sheet, standards have evolved into communications documents that build brand awareness and make it easy to consistently present and promote a company. Now even the smallest company can provide streamlined standards and electronic templates.

Choosing a format should be based on a clear understanding of the audience. The best companies build awareness of their guidelines internally with employees and externally with creative firms. Building a brand, for many companies, is progressively viewed as the shared responsibility of each and every employee.

Characteristics of the best online branding tools

These characteristics were developed by Monigle Associates.

Educational, user-friendly, efficient

Accessible to internal and external users

Builds brand awareness

Consolidates all brand management into one place

Scalable and modular

Positive return on investment contribution

Database-driven, not PDFs

Provides brand resources—signatures, templates, etc.

Always current: new content and functions can be added to improve implementation of the brand

Builds transactional elements into site, i.e., online ordering improves implementation and lowers costs simultaneously

Flexible in hosting and ongoing maintenance

Provides more rather than less information and resources

Online branding tools

The web has made it easy to consolidate brand management into one place that gives employees and vendors user-friendly tools to brand resources. External vendors and creative firms are assigned passwords to access signatures and templates. When the site is used for online ordering or for downloading an image library, the investment usually has a high return.

Design Trust redesigned The Branding Zone, Ernst & Young's brand management extranet that provides graphic standards and templates, education resources and a downloadable image library to 77,000 employees in 130 countries, as well as select agency vendors. To help employees become brand savvy, an interactive branding quiz was developed. When employees answer 80% of the questions correctly, they can download a Global Brand Ambassador certificate.

Branding guides

More and more companies are creating tools that can be easily disseminated to each employee, either to announce the compelling reasons for a new identity and to build awareness of the company brand, and its importance to the future and success of the company.

Crosby Associates designed an elegant ten-panel brochure for Jenner & Block that begins with the firm's mission and its values and displays how the brand is expressed through a variety of marketing communication channels. The format is streamlined, the execution is at the highest level, and it demonstrates rather than declares the value that the company places on its brand.

WGBH disseminated to all its employees a passport-sized brochure titled *WGBH Branding Guidelines*. The brochure's goal is to "take advantage of the wide recognition and powerful positive associations people have with the WGBH brandmark in all of our activities and links with the outside world." This user-friendly guide helps employees more effectively manage WGBH brand assets and also defines branding and other brand terms. It's a cost-effective tool that underscores the fact that everyone plays a role in building the brand.

Marketing and sales toolkits

Companies that have independent distributors and dealerships need effective ways to control the look and feel at the point of sale. VSA Partners has created standards and marketing resources for Harley-Davidson that help independent dealerships achieve a distinctive and memorable retail presence through their exterior signage, retail displays, and advertising.

Thought books

When Pentagram met with Citigroup's global advertising agency and global signage design firm, they presented a thought book that communicated the central unifying principles of the program. Pentagram believe that this encouraged the highest degree of flexibility and creativity in the future. The thought book was an 11-by-17 wire-bound booklet designed to inspire.

Identity standards manuals

Traditionally produced in offset printing, smaller companies are beginning to produce limited-edition manuals using laser printers. Although correct color is usually not attainable, the spirit of the program can be communicated effectively. The binder format allows changes to be made by replacing or adding pages.

Identity standards CDs

The CD, with its large storage capacity and portable format, is a great solution for those companies that can't yet justify putting their standards online. Many companies are putting standards into a PDF format on a CD. It's easy to produce and cost-effective.

Brinker Capital, an investment firm, needed a smart standards program to disseminate to a small group of their agencies and creative firms. A limited-edition CD was produced by Rev Group that will be updated annually as the company grows and its needs evolve. The CD includes everything from business papers and marketing tools to trade show booths.

Designing, specifying, ordering, and printing or fabricating elements of a new brand identity system are all dependent on a set of intelligent standards and guidelines. Good solid standards save time, money, and frustration. The size and nature of an organization affect the depth and breadth of the content and how marketing materials are conceived and produced in the future.

Following is an in-depth composite that can be used as a general reference for building an outline. Usually printing and fabrication specifications accompany design specifications. Legal and nomenclature guideline considerations are critical to include. Some guidelines include order forms for business cards and other applications.

Contents

Companies who value design, and value the contributions of designers, get more effective, strategic, and intelligent marketing and communications solutions. Many companies believe that greater control, efficiency, and cost savings may be garnered through bringing creative work—design, writing, and production—in-house. Brand identity programs are more often than not developed by outside firms who have the experience, staffing, and qualifications to develop new branding strategies. In-house designers often implement the bulk of an identity program once it has been launched and standards are in place.

Understanding the role that the internal design department will play in implementing and managing a new brand identity is critical to the success of the program. The new brand identity is an asset that needs to be managed and nurtured. First and foremost, the identity system itself must be easy to understand and to implement. The balance between consistency and flexibility must be clear at the outset.

Coordinating the identity program standards between the external identity firm and the internal design department is a valuable use of time. The new program and its rationale must be introduced to the internal team, who should have access to the external firm for questions, clarifications, and unforeseen circumstances. The linchpin for implementation is the project manager—the person who coordinates the identity program between the external design firm and the internal design resources. The project manager should have tremendous management and organizational skills, as well as a proven ability to work with creative teams. Another good investment is to bring in the external firm for periodic implementation reviews.

WGBH recognized that design needed to be a function that reported directly to the CEO.

Chris Pullman, Vice President of Design, WGBH

Essential characteristics of in-house design departments

1 Valued by senior management

2 Staffed by experienced designers (creative and technical expertise)

3 Well managed (managed by a creative or design director)

4 Multi-functional (experience across all media)

5 Multi-level experience (senior level and junior level)

6 Open channels of communication with senior management

7 Clearly defined roles and responsibilities for staff members

8 Clearly defined and proven processes and procedures for producing work

9 Commitment to brand identity standards and vision

10 Ability to design with creativity and innovation within system

11 Ability explain the rationale behind design solutions

12 Teamwork; open and clear communication within the group and beyond it

Biggest challenges to in-house design

1 Overcoming political hurdles

2 Getting access to senior management

3 Getting senior management respect for in-house design

4 Overcoming design-by-committee thinking/actions

5 Focusing on high quality rather than the bottom line

6 Debunking the myth that high quality means high cost

7 Getting hands-on designers access to external design firms when developing standards (e.g. design firm develops something that cannot be produced in-house because the two parties did not talk)

8 Too much work for too small a staff

Chris Pullman, WGBH vice president of design, developed this chart to communicate the role of design at WGBH Boston.

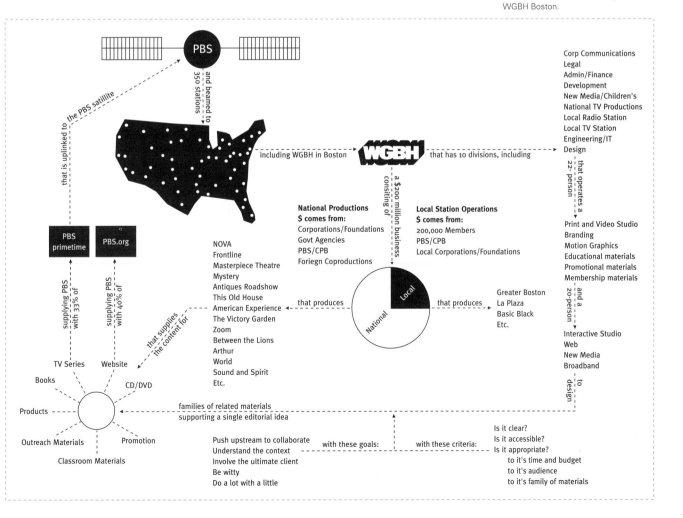

129

Engaging employees in the meaning of the brand and the thinking behind it is one of the best investments that a company can make. Organizational development consultants have long known that long-term success is directly influenced by the way employees share in their company's culture—its values, stories, symbols, and heroes. Traditionally the CEO and the marketing department were the most visible brand champions—individuals who understood and could articulate a company's core values, vision, and brand essence. Enlisting employees as brand champions builds on the underlying concept of aligning culture, behavior, and performance.

"It's not just values, it's the extensive sharing of them that makes a difference," say Terrence Deal and Allan Kennedy in *Corporate Cultures: The Rites and Rituals of Corporate Life.* Companies all around the world are beginning to develop compelling ways of sharing the brand essence—from road shows to online branding tools and guides, to special events. What was once a standards and guidelines tool kit for creative firms has evolved into a brand-building tool for all employees.

Branding is a journey, not a destination.

Andrew Welch, Landor Associates

How an online brand resource center can help build a brand

Developed by Monigle Associates

Communicates strategies and objectives for the brand in an organization

Provides help and best practices as opposed to rules (tools, not rules)

Saves users time

Provides resources people need to participate in the brand-building process

Pulls together often disparate subjects into one online resource center

Tracks user activity to help support future investments

Can reengineer many costly processes, reducing cost from strategy to implementation

Builds consistent implementation

Demystifies brand and identity systems

ARAMARK and the road show

Public companies routinely use road shows to bring their messages directly to key investors and analysts. It is also an effective tactic for launching brand initiatives. ARAMARK Chairman and CEO Joe Neubauer traveled to seven cities to speak to 5,000 front line managers to launch his company's new brand and to align employees with the vision of the company. "If employees are excited and mobilized, then more than half the branding battle has been won," said Bruce Berkowitz, former director of advertising for ARAMARK. "Employees carry the company's culture and character into the marketplace."

ARAMARK worked with a meeting planning company to produce a one-hour road show. The show included a skit performed by Broadway actors and a multimedia presentation of the political, cultural, and economic milestones that gave a context for the company's metamorphosis. Neubauer reinforced key messages about the company's heritage and its leadership in the industry. His overarching message, "Employees are the heart of our success and convey our company's top-tier delivery of services," was supported by a new brandmark. Designed by the Schechter Group (now part of Interbrand) the mark embodies the star quality of the employees and supports the new brand promise of "managed services, managed better."

Managers were fully prepped on the new brand vision and strategy. They received an "Ambassadors Kit" that contained a company history, copies of the new advertising campaign, a merchandise catalogue, and a graphic standards manual. In addition the materials included a manager's checklist and a media launch schedule with explicit instructions on how to handle the launch, how to explain it to staff members, and how to implement the brand identity change. The CEO's presence and passion combined with accessible brand building tools was a powerful combination that fueled ARAMARK's growth.

ARAMARK: Schecter Group

Nickelodeon and the *Orange Book*

Nickelodeon, a global children's entertainment brand owned by Viacom, had grown organically and exponentially over a fifteen-year period. Numerous new brand extensions seen on televison, online, and in feature films, products, and publishing made the brand progressively more disjointed. After extensive interviewing from the company president to a mail clerk, as well as brand analysis, and audits, Adams Morioka, a brand identity firm, presented a master plan for the brand in which the future internal structure would be organized by media. The presentation evolved into the *Nickelodeon Orange Book,* which was made available to everyone in the network. The book outlines core beliefs and values, the internal organization, and the relationship of brand extensions. It includes a flexible and simplified toolkit to keep the focus on clear, simple messages and to inspire creativity. "We want to make the brand more accessible and less mysterious to anyone and everyone involved in Nickelodeon," said Sean Adams, principal, Adams Morioka.

WGBH mission statement and video

The mission statement of WGBH, the Boston affiliate of the Public Broadcasting System, can easily be found on its website and is frequently seen in the signature block of employee e-mail. It reads as follows: "WGBH enriches people's lives through programs and services that educate, inspire, and entertain, fostering citizenship and culture, the joy of learning, and the power of diverse perspectives."

A prominent and easily accessible mission statement is a simple tool that creates a sense of purpose and keeps employees focused on the vision. On the website, the mission statement is followed by a list of commitments that present the unified values of the WGBH. In the "About Us" section, a QuickTime video describes the station as a window on the world and a storyteller to the nation, and cites its commitment to lifelong learning. When internal messages are aligned with external expression, the brand synergy created is evident and the result is profound.

Once the work has been done to create a brand identity, a system needs to be put in place to carry it into the future. As tedious as it may seem, the management of the digital files will profoundly affect how successfully the brand identity is applied after the initial launch. An asset management system must take into consideration all the elements of the brand identity, as well as file naming, formats, organization, storage, retrieval, and overall usability. The designer's responsiblity is to test all files in numerous formats and to develop a system that is logical and sustainable.

Maintaining the quality of reproduction in a world where the tools are constantly changing and where everyone's understanding of digital files, quality, and color is widely disparate is an ongoing challenge. Users will potentially include internal design departments, ad agencies, and members of the sales force creating PowerPoint presentations on their laptops.

More and more people are using digital content. We live at a time when digital files have become democratic in a sense—PC and Mac users, professionals from all walks of life, download and use these files every day to communicate, sell, persuade, and present. It is not unusual anymore to be able to go into the media section of a website and download logos, images, and templates.

The typical user fails to find a desired file 39% of the time.

Media Asset Management Report 2002, Gistics

File Format Matrix

To insure optimum reproduction of a logo, be sure to use one of the recommended file formats for the software you are using.

Software	.bmp	.cgm	.eps	.gif	.jpg	.tif	.wmf
Adobe Illustrator			●		○	○	
Macromedia Freehand			●				
Adobe Pagemaker		○	●			○	○
Adobe Photoshop			●	○	○	○	
CorelDRAW			●	○	○	○	
Microsoft Excel	○	●	●	○	○	○	○
Microsoft Word		○	●		○	○	●
Microsoft PowerPoint		○	○		●	●	○
WordPerfect			●				
QuarkXPress			●			○	○

○ Acceptable   Developed by Monigle Associates
● Recommended

File Naming

Files should be named as concisely and informatively as possible so they can be understood at a glance. Consistency is imperative for grouping common attributes and distinguishing unique ones.

File Format Basics

Different image file formats are appropriate to specific publishing circumstances.

Vector Graphics

Vector graphics are digital images created in drawing applications such as Adobe Illustrator, Macromedia Freehand, and CorelDRAW. Because they are based on mathematically defined lines and curves, they can be manipulated and scaled without losing reproduction quality.

Vector graphics use the Encapsulated PostScript (EPS) format.

Raster or Bitmap Graphics

Raster or bitmap graphics are digital images created, captured or edited in applications such as Adobe Photoshop. Because they are constructed as a continuous mapping of pixels, the image cannot be scaled, rotated, or skewed outside of a image-editing application without the loss of reproduction quality.

Examples of raster or bitmap image file types are:

EPS—An Encapsulated PostScript file can contain vector and/or bitmap graphics. An EPS file is the preferred file format used for offset printing and with high-end output devices. EPS files will provide the highest-quality output and should be used in-house when printing to a printer equipped with or compatible with Adobe PostScript.

TIFF—Used for in-house printing when a PostScript output device is unavailable (i.e., inkjet printers without Adobe PostScript). TIFFs are convenient for exchanging image files between computer platforms.

GIF—A compressed file format used to display graphics and images in HTML for on-screen viewing.

JPEG—A compressed file format used to display continuous-tone images such as photographs in HTML for on-screen viewing.

BMP—A Windows-compatible bit-mapped image file format that allows users to place, view, and laser-print graphics from their desktop.

The following case studies illustrate a broad range of branding and identity scenarios from the public, private, and retail sectors. The organizations range in size and mission—from local community-based initiatives to some of the largest corporations in the world. The nature of the problems solved is also diverse: from creating a unique persona for a new company to repositioning an existing brand. Mergers and acquisitions present yet another level of complexity and challenge.

The firms represent a range of methodologies and size. From branding and design consultancies to multidisciplinary design firms, the common denominator is the excellence of the work, and the responsible process that each office used to achieve its goals. Each office demonstrated an unswerving commitment to solving the client's problem with a sustainable and intelligent solution. Each program featured is unique, memorable, and differentiated.

Case study variables

Size of the organization

Nature of the problem

Complexity of the problem

Challenge of the engagement

Length of the engagement

Philosophy of the brand identity firm

Size of the firm

Decision-making process

Number of decision makers

Evolution

Tate
Four museums
Wolff Olins
London

FedEx
Global courier
Landor Associates
San Francisco

**Brooklyn Academy
of Music**
Performing-arts venue
Pentagram
New York

Amazon.com
Retailer
Turner Duckworth
San Francisco

Harley-Davidson
Motorcycle company
VSA Partners
Chicago

Chicago GSB
Business school
Crosby Associates
Chicago

Presbyterian Church
Religious organization
Malcolm Grear Associates
Providence

**Franklin Institute
Science Museum**
Educational institution
Allemann Almquist & Jones
Philadelphia

Zoom
Children's TV program
WGBH
Boston

Mobil
Petroleum company
Chermayeff & Geismar
New York

Census 2000
Government campaign
Two Twelve Associates
Sylvia Harris
New York

Merger

BP
Petroleum company
Landor Associates
London

Cingular Wireless
Telecommunications
VSA Partners
Chicago

Citi
Financial services
Pentagram
New York

Pharmacia
Pharmaceutical
Crosby Associates
Chicago

Bank of America
Financial services
Enterprise IG
New York

Creating the New

Sanctum
Web security
Frankfurt Balkind
New York

Tazo
Tea products
Sandstrom Design
Portland

**Martha Stewart Living
Omnimedia**
Lifestyle retailer
MSLO
Doyle Partners
New York

92
Restaurant
Louise Fili, Ltd.
New York

**White House Conference
for Children**
Government forum
Chermayeff & Geismar
New York

Center City District
Civic association
Joel Katz Design Associates
Philadelphia

Foodsource
Specialty supermarket
Bonita Albertson
Philadelphia

From an imposing nineteenth-century edifice in central London to a collection housed in a former power station on the Thames, from a modern museum on the southwest coast of England to a museum housed in a converted warehouse in the north, the galleries that constitute the Tate Collections are as different from each other as their architecture.

By the late '90s, Tate had become three galleries (London Millbank, Liverpool, and St. Ives). Each had a different focus, and with a fourth gallery due to open on London Bankside in 2000, the time was right to clarify the picture. In transitioning Tate from an institution-led to a brand-led organization, Tate retained Wolff Olins to work on the creation of a new brand that would unify the collections and the four sites. At the heart of the project was the idea of "one Tate, yet many Tates."

Tate wanted to enhance its appeal and tap the potential for substantially increasing its audience. It also wanted to establish a more forward-thinking and accessible approach to art—in essence, taking art off the pedestal and making it available to everyone without dumbing it down. In addition, Tate's leadership was open to the idea of redefining what a museum might be.

Wolff Olins worked closely with Sir Nicholas Serota, the Tate's director, and his communications staff to drive and manage the branding process. Wolff Olins conducted extensive interviews across departments and levels to clearly define Tate's opportunity and ambition. Additionally, Tate had conducted research on both visitors and nonvisitors and learned, for example, that in the United Kingdom, more people now visited museums than attended football matches.

Wolff Olins' central brand idea, "Look again, think again," was conceived to be an invitation to visitors to reconsider what the experience of a gallery is like as well as to be a challenge to the staff to reevaluate the way art is presented. "This vision served not only to reposition Tate, but also has changed attitudes toward art galleries and museums," said Brian Boylan, chairman of Wolff Olins. "The Tate experience is about culture and art, and entertainment and enjoyment."

The new brand strategy simplified the names of the four museums while strengthening the institution's identity. The museum had been previously referred to as "the Tate," but Wolff Olins dropped the definite article. What was known as the Tate Gallery or London Millbank became Tate Britain. The other museums became Tate Modern, Tate Liverpool, and Tate St. Ives. This strategy helps distinguish the locations for visitors and positions Tate on a more global scale.

Brand values   **Brand applications**   Brand toolkit   Contact us

The Tate brand identity is alive. It allows freedom to be expressive, to be appropriate to subject or event.
Always fresh, but always clearly from Tate.

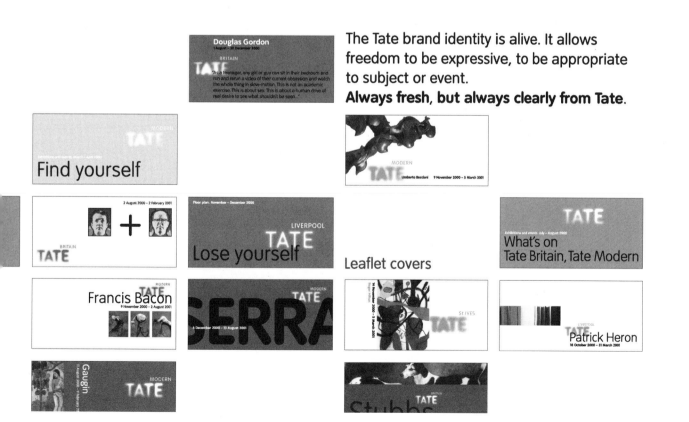

The use of the brand allows flexibility within a unified identity. Instead of one unchanging symbol in a prescribed color consistently applied across all media, Wolff Olins created four dynamic and futuristic wordmarks to be used interchangeably, each in a different stage of metamorphosis. Each is based on the name "Tate" in caps, but each one appears to be at a different level of focus. The design conveys transformation and nonconformity. Fluidity of form reflects the essence of Tate's point of view, because the identity is always changing—from the illuminated signage atop Tate Modern to the front and back of the gift bags to the coffee cups in the café. "A successful brand is all about detail. Every facet of a brand must be apparent in an organization's communications, behavior, products and environment," Boylan said.

Great identities inspire a range of descriptions and interpretations. An information assistant at Tate Modern described the identity as a "bright light that expresses the spirit and values of Tate. The four versions communicate that Tate is a place where new ideas are constantly being shown. The ever-changing colors reflect a vision for a changing future," she said.

Everything that Tate does is designed to take art to a wider audience. Large billboards are hung in Turbine Hall of Tate Modern to advertise existing and forthcoming exhibitions. Illuminated exhibition signage at Tate Modern can be read from across the Thames, and exhibition banners hang ceremoniously between the columns at Tate Britain. Tate's luminous and expansive color palette is unpredictable and fresh in its hues and values. Wolff Olins also designed a unique typeface called Tate for the interior signage system, which is also used in all signatures and exhibition signage. An online brand toolkit ensures that the many designers and agencies involved with Tate are in sync with the vision.

In the year prior to opening of Tate Modern in spring 2000, the Tate galleries recorded a combined total of 4 million visitors. Between 2000 and 2001, the visitor figures to the newly branded Tate Britain, Tate Modern, Tate Liverpool, and Tate St. Ives rose to 7.5 million. In 2002, in keeping with a strategy to redefine what a museum could be, Tate announced a radical new location, Tate in Space, designed to orbit our planet. Collaboration has begun between architects, space scientists, engineers, artists, Tate curators, conservators, and art handlers.

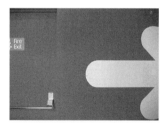

It's almost impossible to imagine life without FedEx—the revolutionary idea that raised our expectations and changed the way we conduct business. In 1973, fledgling Federal Express Corporation ("FedEx") effectively launched the air express industry by delivering 186 packages overnight to 25 U.S. cities. Today, through the FedEx family of companies over five million packages are delivered each business day to over 200 countries. Along the way, FedEx Express has maintained an operating standard characterized by continuous innovation in technology, from implementing the first PC-based automated shipping system to online package processing and tracking.

In a relationship that began in 1993, Landor Associates has co-created two generations of branding transformations for FedEx. The original identity, Federal Express, was thought to be a potential impediment to building a global business. By the early '90s, the words "FedEx" had entered the vernacular and, unlike the former name, could be said easily by customers who didn't speak English. Landor CEO Clay Timon said, "The consumers themselves had evolved the brand to FedEx. It had become the Kleenex and the Coke of its category." Landor helped FedEx position itself as the world standard for fast and reliable service with its brand line "The World on Time" and launched "FedEx" as the primary verbal and visual identifier. A new bold identity was applied to uniforms, packaging, and fleets of planes and vehicles.

Corporation

Express

Ground

Freight

Custom Critical

Trade Networks

Beginning in 1998, the parent company of FedEx, originally called FDX Corp., began acquiring related companies including RPS, a major handler of small ground packages, Viking Freight, Caliber Logistics, Roberts Express, American Freightways, and others. Each company was a well-regarded operating company and retained its own brand name. Collectively, they made possible a group of companies that could provide a broad spectrum of transportation, supply chain and information system services.

Fred Smith, the founder, chairman and CEO began to formulate a vision for the 21st century based on a common information interface for all global customers that provided one brand link to a broad spectrum of transportation and logistics service. Peter Wise, Landor relationship leader, said, "We began to examine new brand architecture and verbal branding solutions that would make it simpler for customers and prospects to understand the global scope of FedEx and its range of capabilities.

Landor worked with the FedEx brand leaders to update core brand attributes, which supported the future vision. The new brand architecture unified the independent operating companies under the powerful FedEx brand, accompanied by clear language to differentiate each company service: FedEx Express, FedEx Ground, FedEx Freight, FedEx Custom Critical, and FedEx Trade Networks. Each operating company was also color-coded. This approach had several strategic advantages. Not only was it aligned with Fred Smith's vision and requirements to build highly independent companies that could collectively compete under a strong global brand, but the unified brand symbolized one convenient touchpoint for all customers regardless of their need or location.

This radical change was indeed risky, since conversion to the new brand architecture involved a large capital investment during a period of complex organizational and technological changes. And it involved extension of the hugely valuable FedEx brand into new areas of service and operations. But, Wise explained, "You become a breakaway brand by taking risks. The best strategies emerge from leadership that has confidence in their vision, point of view and experience."

FedEx brand attributes

Simplifying

It's easy to work with FedEx. We don't waste anyone's time. Our procedures are straightforward, and our communications are clear.

Optimizing

Every FedEx customer has different needs. We find the right solution and the right price—for each customer's business.

Certain

Our customers don't have time for "almost." They demand certainty. FedEx delivers.

Personal

FedEx customers are people, not transactions. We get to know each customer and offer him or her the tools they need to achieve their goals.

Inventive

Global business constantly changes. So does FedEx. As we invent new solutions, we lead the way in operations, technology, and e-commerce.

Connecting

FedEx makes connections. Our networks link people, packages, and information around the clock and around the world.

Major FedEx branding decisions are usually made by the chairman/CEO, the VP of marketing, and the director of global brand management. "The success of FedEx branding has been driven by smart instinct, swift decision-making and compelling execution, with the role of research often being to validate and provide executional guidance," says Gayle Christensen, FedEx managing director of brand management.

Landor proceeded to develop a comprehensive Brand Resource Management tool for FedEx. "We believe that it is the most robust online brand management resource in the world," Wise said. "It is designed to make the core meaning of the brand resonate with all employees and key partners. The user interface is designed to engage the user with the brand attributes." With over 3,000 downloads, the website houses the brand assets of all FedEx operating companies. Another feature is a Global Brand Management feedback and approval loop—when a brochure or other print literature is designed and submitted, it is tested against the core brand attributes, and the sponsoring manager receives feedback within 36 hours.

"It's hard to be the center of the world when you are in Brooklyn," said Michael Bierut, a partner at Pentagram, about his client, the Brooklyn Academy of Music. Founded in 1885, it is the oldest continuously operating performing-arts venue in the United States. In the 1960s, Harvey Lichtenstein, a dancer, natural-born impresario, and visionary, had an unerring knack for countering the programs of Lincoln Center and Carnegie Hall. He inaugurated the Next Wave Festival and brought in avant-garde performances from around the world. He figured out what else people would come to Brooklyn to see, from Laurie Anderson to Zingaro (a ballet on horseback) and Philip Glass and *Einstein on the Beach*. He created a tradition of the new and an aura of hip.

Lichtenstein also made a splash in the design community and hired the most cutting-edge graphic designers. Like the majority of not-for-profit institutions, BAM hired the best design talent for high-visibility pieces, and everything else was produced higgledy-piggledy with an eye on cost.

In 1998, the new marketing director realized that all the publicity and marketing efforts were too fragmented and confused subscribers. Since the Next Wave

Festival had become a recognizable and trusted brand, it was decided to build BAM's entire brand around it. BAM approached Pentagram to figure it out. They thought they needed a new umbrella identity that would encompass all performance venues. The client delivered cardboard boxes filled with hundreds of pieces—from programs to half-page newspaper ads, tickets, postcards, direct mail, and fund-raising solicitations.

Michael Bierut instinctively knew that "BAM needed more than a logo to put people in the seats." His design strategy was to create a bold identity system and style that could always work. His recommendation was very simple: "No matter what you are communicating about, no matter what medium it is, no matter what size, no matter how many colors, you are going to use these horizontal bars and you are going to have one typeface. The horizontal bars are always going to interrupt the large type, which will always be News Gothic."

Everyone involved on the marketing committee loved it but said, "Harvey is going to want to know why." In response, Bierut answered, "It's about showing that BAM is transgressive—it crosses boundaries and it's over the horizon."

Pentagram designed a bold visual language that was simple in concept, distinctive, dramatically differentiated from other performance venues, and easy to execute. "The advantage of interrupting the type is that you get scale and monumentality without the real estate that it actually takes to achieve scale and monumentality. We let it play out—always the stripes, always the interrupted typefaces. And no matter what we tried, it worked." And no matter what customers received in the mail, they saw the interrupted type and knew immediately that it was BAM.

Pentagram was then asked to do a special piece on Baroque opera and discovered that the interruptions actually worked using other typefaces, such as Snell Round. Changing the variables still worked. A very smart and supportive board member who was a corporate marketing director said, "Let's stop fooling around. Let's just always use the same typeface." Bierut admitted that the board member was right, and remarked, "The best thing that you can have is a backlog of experience to guide you, and the willingness to make mistakes now and then, the humility to admit it, and to retrench."

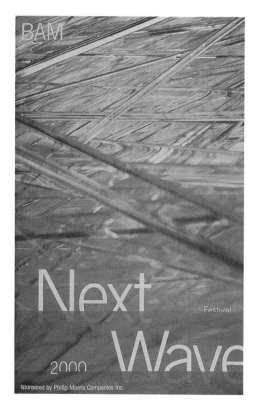

Brochure by BAMdesign's Jason Ring

Brochure by BAMdesign's Eric Olson

Bierut developed a one-page identity standards mantra so that BAM's in-house art department could take over. Some of them had been Bierut's students at Yale. The innovative young designers embraced the visual language and proceeded to take the program in dynamic new directions—finding new ways to extend the essence and keep it fresh and surprising.

External signage was the next frontier. Building on the concept of interruption, Bierut found a way to merge the contemporary BAM language with the Beaux Arts language of a majestic opera house. Two years after the initial system design, Bierut designed a new mark for BAM, a square with the acronym interrupted. "We could have never started here. We would have failed. We needed to begin at the numerous points of communication."

Bierut continues to be a design adviser to BAM. Designing a bold and sustainable system for a not-for-profit that he believes in is a Pentagram signature.

Amazon.com will always be considered the e-commerce company that changed the future of retailing forever. Originally conceived as the place to buy books, it is now positioned as the "Web's biggest retail store." By 1999, Amazon.com had expanded its offerings to include music, software, toys, tools, electronics, and housewares. Founded in 1994 and initially operated out of the founder's garage, the company now has over thirty million customers and ships to more than 150 countries.

In 1999, Amazon.com retained Turner Duckworth to redesign its brand identity. The mandate was to convey that "Amazon.com was more than just a place to buy books. . . it's a place to buy anything and everything." Positioning as a customer-focused, friendly company was core to the company's mission and values. The challenge was to create a unique and proprietary identity that maintained what Amazon.com felt were its brand equities: the recognition of lower-case type in the logo, and the appearance of the orange swoosh underneath the word.

Turner Duckworth immersed itself in the brand, spent a lot of time on Amazon.com, and examined competitor sites. The firm also analyzed what makes a logo effective or ineffective on the web.

"Our goal was to infuse personality into the logo, and to create a compelling idea that would convey the brand message," said David Turner, head of design. The design team developed distinct visual strategies at the first stage—each one emphasized a different aspect of the positioning brief.

The final logo design was an evolutionary leap from the old logo. The central idea behind the new logo reflected the client's business strategy of selling more than just books. The design team connected the initial *a* of "amazon" to the *z*. This approach clearly communicated "Amazon.com sells everything from A to Z." The graphic

amazon.com

device that connects the *a* and the *z* also speaks to the brand positioning, which was largely customer-focused and friendly service. This device forms a cheeky smile with a dimple that pushes up the *z*. The brown shipper box packaging was considered at every stage of the logo design.

Turner Duckworth designed custom lettering for the wordmark, and made the "amazon" more prominent than the ".com." The typography was designed to give the logo a friendlier and more unique look. The design team also designed a full alphabet so that Amazon.com could update its international domains, presently in the United Kingdom, Germany, France, and Japan. The project was completed in eight weeks.

Jeff Bezos, the CEO, founder, and visionary, was involved at every presentation and was the key decision maker. "Access to the key decision maker, and in particular to the visionary of a company, certainly makes our work easier. Not only does it accelerate the feedback, development and approval processes, but it also allows us to ask questions of the visionary and hear unedited answers," said Joanne Chan, head of client services.

Amazon.com had determined that it would execute a "soft launch" of the new identity. The new brand identity was not announced to the press or highlighted on its website. Sensitive to the perceptions of customers and Wall Street analysts, the company felt it was important that Amazon.com didn't appear to be a "different" company.

"At times, a creative brief may describe brand values that are more aspirational goals than reality. At Amazon.com, it was clear that the focus and attitude of the company and its employees truly matched and set the standard for its brand values. The focus on customer service—and in particular friendly, accessible service—was clearly reflected in the work ethic and practice of the CEO himself and his marketing team," remarked Chan.

Why did you name your company "Amazon?"

"Earth's biggest river. Earth's biggest selection."
Jeff Bezos, founder and CEO

In 1903, William S. Harley, age twenty one, and Arthur Davidson, age twenty, made the first production Harley-Davidson motorcycle available to the public. From their small wooden shed with the name Harley-Davidson scrawled on the floor, one doubts they could have imagined that, a century later, more than 250,000 riders would gather to celebrate the company's 100th anniversary. Nor would they have been able to imagine "The Art of the Motorcycle," the 1998 show at the Guggenheim Museum, where riders who brought their motorcycles to Fifth Avenue and Ninety-second Street entered free.

"Corners feel like choreography. Mind, body, and machine work as one," says the *Rider's Edge* course book for first-time motorcycle riders. An appreciation for that experience probably best characterizes Harley-Davidson's eclectic ridership, which crosses cultures, genders, and demographics, unified by a passion for riding, for living, and for the motorcycle itself. The H-D brand today is equated with freedom, independence, and individualism.

But in 1981, it was a very different case. The company had lost its focus and was hemorrhaging red ink. That year, thirteen H-D executives bought the company back from AMF. The new leadership set about to reinvent the business from both an operating and engineering stance. One significant asset left intact was the intense loyalty and nearly evangelistic fervor customers felt for the product. Management realized if they focused their internal resources around these intangibles, the resulting efforts would change their guiding philosophy and the business. The team proceeded to focus on creating leaders within the organization, establishing a set of core values and unrivaled product quality. Rank-and-file employees, along with executives, hit the road to share their beliefs with customers worldwide. This way of life at Harley-Davidson has redefined the meaning of "being close to the customer."

By the year 2000, H.O.G. (Harley Owners Group) had half a million members, making it the largest factory-sponsored motorcycle club in the world.

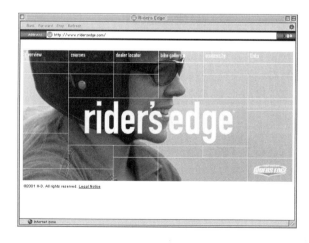

"Branding can be approached as a positioning science or as an organizational movement. Harley-Davidson chose to build its brand from the inside out, fueling the effort with immense passion from employees, dealers, and customers," said Dana Arnett, principal, VSA Partners. As a result, H-D has achieved legend status as a company that has leveraged branding as a growth driver of the business.

VSA Partners began working with Harley-Davidson in 1985. Arnett said, "We are one cog in a large machine that has helped reignite the brand over the years, from a host of amazing employees to David Aaker, the marketing strategist, and Carmichael Lynch," H-D's advertising agency for the past twenty years. Harley-Davidson has found a way to meld product quality and innovation with the customer experience, which has resulted in steady profitable growth.

What differentiates Harley-Davidson from most companies is that the employees live the brand in all they do. The fact that they too are customers creates a circle of sustainability, as the entire organization believes in and lives the customer experience. Employees participate in rallies with customers and spend time with dealers. The idea of participation also can be seen in H-D's relationships with its advertising agency, design firm, and architectural firms. At VSA Partners, for example, most of the creative team on the H-D account ride motorcycles. "While it's not a required rite of passage, living inside the motorcycle experience informs our decision-making process and keeps us aware of the reality of what will and what will not fly," said Arnett.

Harley-Davidson competes on an emotional level, which is supported by a laserlike focus on the "look, sound, and feel." Not many companies can claim customers who tattoo the company logo on their bodies. And while other companies trademark colors, H-D registered the sound of its 45-degree, overhead-valve, air-cooled V-Twin engine, but withdrew the request after more than a year of responding to competitors' protests.

Superior design has been an essential element of Harley-Davidson's strategy. "The way H-D embodies design is endemic to the way they do business. From the design of the V-Rod to their leather jackets to the architecture of their factories, design honors the origins and the character of the company," said Arnett. During their long relationship, VSA Partners has worked on a wide range of brand initiatives from the marketing of customized parts and accessories, which is a key contributor to the H-D revenue stream, to jump-starting their online presence. VSA has worked closely with the H-D environmental design team to help transform the retail experience and has designed licensed products, books, and annual reports. "You could say that we've been active in the showroom, the boardroom, and all points between," said Arnett.

Continuity with the creative team builds a platform of trust and respect, from which truly creative ideas can emerge. "Both Carmichael Lynch and VSA Partners have been working with H-D for many, many years. There is a complete and implicit understanding of what is going to work. A very big part of our success is that H-D supports all of its relationships with active participation. Important to our process is the iterative and relevant course of dialogue. We have real conversations about real issues that are affecting the company and the marketplace. We talk about how products behave and the emotions one experiences with a Harley. There's also a level of trust and candor when we engage with this client—it's as if I am conversing with my colleagues," said Arnett.

Successful public companies manage for growth and marketplace demand, but they also focus on delivering a believable story that investors can rely on. Leadership's ability to crystallize "who they are" and "who they want to be" for all employees and customers has made H-D into a highly recognizable brand whose equity transcends the balance sheet. "They are an American icon," said Arnett.

Brands that withstand the test of time are inevitably truthful and genuine.

Dana Arnett, principal, VSA Partners

Rider's Edge®

The median age of Harley buyers is now 44 and for Buell buyers it's 39. Yet, half of both Harley-Davidson and competitive brand owners entered the sport between the ages of 15 and 29.

VSA Partners created a CD-ROM toolkit with marketing resources for Harley-Davidson's independent dealerships that included advertising, retail displays, and exterior signage.

The business of business schools is to develop leaders who will transform the future of business. "While many institutions teach you what to think, our graduate program delivers a rigorous transformation in the very way you think," said the dean of the University of Chicago Graduate School of Business. The school proudly claims more Nobel laureates among faculty and alumni than any other business school in the nation. Approximately one hundred years after its founding, the graduate school retained Crosby Associates to develop a comprehensive visual identity and branding program.

The school had created volumes of research-based studies that Crosby distilled into a positioning document that clearly defined the program goals, brand position, and problems that needed resolution. From extensive interviews conducted with various deans, professors, and administrators, Crosby found numerous names used to identify the institution. The school's long name was frequently transposed, and the shortened versions ranged from just "Chicago" to "The GSB." The University of Chicago Graduate School of Business was one of the few top-tier MBA schools that did not have a simple, one-word communicative name, such as Tuck, Wharton, or Stanford. "These single names become powerful identifiers and differentiators both in verbal and visual communications," said Bart Crosby, principal.

Crosby's strategy was not to change the formal name of the esteemed institution but rather to determine an informal verbal and visual identifier that would best satisfy the goal of having a single, manageable, and more recognizable brand. "Competition at business schools is always increasing. A stronger brand name will increase awareness and facilitate effective communications through prominent and consistent use."

The ultimate goal of the program was "to make the GSB the most highly respected business school brand among those audiences who are ultimately critical to the school's success." Crosby presented seven informal name candidates that were already in use. In the presentation, each name was isolated and applied as hypothetical signage on the dominant building on campus. Each candidate was then analyzed for its positive and negative connotations both in the academic environment and the larger world of business leadership.

The final name that was recommended was Chicago GSB. "It is the most logical choice because it follows the sequence of the institution's formal name." said Crosby. Chicago GSB would now become the official wordmark, and act as the primary verbal and visual identifier. Chicago GSB would never stand alone, however—it would always be accompanied by the complete, official name. The names of programs, centers, institutes, and publications would remain the same in the new system but be secondary. The only logo allowed would be the Chicago GSB logotype.

In the extensive print and electronic communications audit, Crosby found little differentiation from other MBA programs, relatively low visibility compared to peer institutions, and a lack of collective impact and consistency. There were no official signatures with the exception of the university shield. "We wanted to increase recognition for the school. Our goal was to visually connect a future orientation with dignity, tradition and the school's core essence," said Crosby.

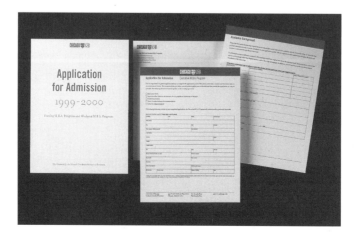

The primary visual element in the identity program is the wordmark, which juxtaposes both bold and elegant typography and frames the university shield, which has been redrawn and simplified. The new shield lends itself to being a large graphic element. Its redrawn features allow it to be printed, hot-stamped, or embossed to add visual texture.

Crosby Associates developed a cohesive identity program that is positioned as intellectual but congenial. "We believe that Chicago GSB's communications should reflect an organization that is prestigious, passionate, and proud, and one that is smart, resourceful, analytical, and ambitious." The formatting system uses a simple, proportional grid system for print and electronic communications. The typefaces for the program, Filosophia, a classic serif font, and Trade Gothic Condensed, a compact, modern font, create a proprietary look and allow for flexibility of use. Comprehensive guidelines were published in a perfect-bound brochure format and are also available on the web. The GSB Publications Office is always available to answer any questions about the program.

Brand Attributes

World-class

Intelligent

Prestigious

Proud

Individualistic

Smart

Congenial but competitive

Resourceful

Rigorous

Innovative

Analytical

Passionate

Ambitious

Having tradition

The Presbyterian Church (USA), with 2.5 million members, 11,200 congregations, and 21,000 pastors in the United States, is governed at all levels by a combination of clergy and church members, both male and female. The church traces its history to the sixteenth century and the Protestant Reformation. The two major branches of the Presbyterian Church that had been separated since the Civil War were united in 1983. It was then the Church decided a new symbol or seal should represent the unified institution.

The eight-person task force, comprised of theologians, pastors, educators, an artist, and a musician, were given the mission to determine what should be in the new seal and conduct a national search for a designer. After interviewing forty-six firms, the task force chose Malcolm Grear Designers.

The task force had extensive theological and philosophical discussions around what symbols and images should be included in the seal. They wanted a seal that would serve as a symbolic statement of the unification as well. "We wanted a design that had an emotive, evocative character, suggesting the vitality of the mission of the church and yet it should be more formal than informal in nature and have a structural or ordered quality," said Dr. John M. Muldar, chair of the task force. The task force provided a list of theological ideas to be incorporated: the cross, fire, the Trinity, the Holy Spirit, and the Word. Malcolm Grear's studio brought in Dr. Martha Gregor Geothals, a historian and artist trained in theology, to give a historical perspective on the history and meaning of Christian symbols.

The task force and the design team formed a close relationship and had numerous discussions around the meaning of symbols and the Presbyterian Church's legacy. What seemed like an impossible goal for any experienced designer started a design process that generated close to four thousand sketches. Initially, Grear was obsessed with finding an answer, but could never develop a design that would incorporate more than three of the theological ideas. "I worked on possibilities all day every day and most of every night. I dreamed about the symbol during whatever time was left to sleep," said Grear. "There was an aura of mystery about this ancient institution that fascinated me," he said. After an exhaustive exploration, he finally was able to incorporate the cross, fire, the descending dove, and the book in the design of the mark.

Grear's recommendation to the diverse task force received unanimous approval, but that was only the first step. The church's charter required that the General Assembly—seven hundred individuals—vote on it. "This struck me as too democratic. I had grandly stated on many occasions that I would not play to a cast of thousands when seeking approval of our designs. But I was in this race to stay," said Grear.

The Cross

The Pulpit

The Fish

The Fire

The Dove

The Cup

The Book

The Triangle

The general assembly staff developed a powerful video presentation of the seal and its meaning. The video's score included two traditional hymns—"Amazing Grace" and "How Firm a Foundation." The assembly gave Grear and Geothals a standing ovation, and the rest is history. It represented the first unanimous vote in the history of the Church. The story of the process was immortalized in a book written by the leader of the task force, and the website contains an in-depth explanation of the meaning of all of the elements. Dr. Muldar has said, "The design has proved to be a simple but eloquent statement of the Presbyterian Church's heritage, identity and mission. . . I have used the seal to teach people the meaning of the Presbyterian tradition, and I have been intrigued by the way the seal itself engages people's imagination. . . it helps them to understand the content and imagery of the Bible and the abstractions of doctrine and theology."

The seal has been applied to an enormous variety of applications—from stained-glass windows and church bulletins to informational signage, needlework, and ties. Almost twenty-years after the initial design, the Presbyterian Church returned to Malcolm Grear Designers to redesign its website and to create branding guidelines for the web.

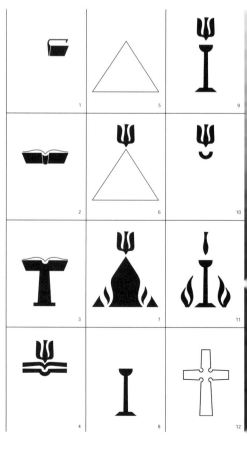

Malcolm Grear's guiding principles

We believe that the art of communicating information, which includes values as well as facts, is essential to successful performance in organizations.

We believe that the creativity which evolves an inspired symbol and message, while elusive, is best nurtured when enthusiastic people with imagination and curiosity immerse themselves in their client's mission.

We believe that sensitive insight and research into the special conditions of each client are needed to discover meaning and to organize information.

We believe that the informative message integrates the verbal and numerative with the pictorial and sculptural.

We believe that imagery must be fresh and appropriate, but it must also be enduring and must sustain long enjoyment in many contexts. Its meaning should never be exhausted immediately.

The Franklin Institute's hands-on approach to science and technology has drawn hundreds of thousands of schoolchildren to its unique historic displays and interactive exhibits each year. From walking through a giant beating human heart, to gazing at the universe at the Fels Planetarium, the museum becomes a life memory for most visitors.

"We need a new identity that will appeal both to schoolchildren and the global scientific community, appropriate to an institution that has a rich 175-year history and a constantly evolving future." That was the essence of the challenge given to Allemann Almquist & Jones. The Franklin Institute was expanding its physical space dramatically to include a Futures Center and an IMAX Theater. It had two personas: the Franklin Institute, its corporate face, and the Franklin Institute Science Museum, its popular face.

The Franklin Institute created a five-member identity steering committee, which included directors and managers of the institution's various divisions. AA&J worked closely with this team over a six-month time period.

Design process

After reviewing its 175-year archive of identities, publications, and promotional campaigns, and experiencing the museum's exhibits, AA&J conducted in-depth interviews with key individuals, from the chairman to the chief scientist and astronomer to the exhibit director, in order to find out more about the aspirations, uniqueness, and culture of the Franklin Institute. AA&J also examined identities of Philadelphia's cultural and entertainment destinations, other institutions that carried the Franklin name, and other science museums around the world. The existing identity was carefully analyzed to determine whether there was any equity that needed to be retained.

After the interview and audit, AA& J determined that the Franklin Institute needed to be positioned as a friendly place where science can be experienced through observation and hands-on interactive play. The identity needed to be contemporary, simple, and timeless, and should appeal to the broadly defined local, national, and international audience. Since the Franklin Institute was brilliant at mixing science and technology with a sense of wonder and fun, AA&J also believed that a sense of magic needed to be conveyed. The identity needed to work on a range of applications from a white paper on chaos theory to a fifty-foot banner and a membership card, and had to take into consideration that a not-for-profit institution always has budget challenges. AA& J recommended that a mark be used as a primary identifier, with a clean and highly legible treatment for the new name.

  **The Franklin Institute Science Museum**

AA&J started the design process with totally schematic studies, looking at how such a long name could function with a mark. The entire design team started examining the broadest range of possibilities for symbols, starting with visual translations of the hands-on theme and various science metaphors. After hundreds of sketches were created, everything went on the wall for an office-wide critique in which content and form were analyzed, tossed, challenged, and rethought. Only the strong survived. AA&J believes that getting distance from the ideas is critical—a studio needs to stop design development in order to determine whether there are any viable, sustainable solutions. Is there a kernel of an idea that needs further exploration?

The process of determining the final solution and reducing a complex idea to its essence requires focus, patience and unending discipline. "The best identity designers have a strong understanding of how to communicate effectively through the use of signs and symbols, have a keen sense of form and letterforms, and an understanding of the history of design," said Hans-U. Allemann, principal and designer.

The final solution was found through exploring hundreds of different ideas. All of a sudden, the solution emerged. "We usually begin with very predictable and obvious ideas, but the beauty of the identity design process is that it is totally unpredictable. We never know what the process will reveal. I have been designing marks for forty years, and the process still astonishes me," said Allemann.

The final mark is a sun within a circle behind a circle. It creates the impression of a sunrise behind a planet symbolizing the future. As one continues to look at it, one senses its ambiguity and layers of meaning. It also conveys the magical and transient moment of an eclipse. It is a sophisticated mark, and yet it is inviting, warm, and immediate. When asked about it, a five-year-old said, "Of course, it's the sun, moon, and earth."

After reviewing and testing various fonts, Futura Bold was selected for the name treatment. This type style was chosen for its high legibility and also because the quality of its letterforms seemed to work well with the mark. The letters, however, were redrawn and modified. Allemann created a ligature between the *T* and *h,* altered the relationships of the cap height to the *x* height, and completely redrew the *M.* This work was critical because it was a very long name, and how it plays out in various scales is crucial in maintaining legibility at various scales. Three modified versions of the mark were also developed to guarantee legibility and quality of reproduction at the wide range of sizes required for applications.

The identity, which was created in the late eighties, continues to be fresh and dynamic. Because of the iconic quality, the mark works at minute scales and as large environmental graphic elements and, like an eclipse, its form can weave in and out of layers of visual information without losing its ability to communicate.

Media visionaries have been talking about the convergence of TV and the web since the early nineties, promising a more personalized, intuitive, and seamless experience. While media moguls continue to brainstorm, the creators and producers at WGBH in Boston have created the broadcast web loop that is achieving off-the-charts feedback, and they've been doing it since 1998. "By kids, for kids" is the essence of *Zoom,* which combines a daily PBS TV show and website with educational outreach into an interactive experience. Programming is created from e-mailed suggestions, the cast is all kids, and each day kids' ideas are posted on the site. Children from the ages of six to eleven are challenged to explore, experiment, and share their creativity in a virtual environment devoid of adults and commercials.

The 278 public television stations that offer *Zoom* reach 92 percent of U.S. television households. In a single week, five million kids watch *Zoom* on TV, 210,000 log on to the website, and 25,000 kids submit ideas via e-mail for new activities, as well as their own scientific results. The website engages kids for an average of 30 minutes per visit, which is well above four times the average. The number of e-mails exceeds any direct marketer's dream.

"Is it zoomy enough?" is the ongoing challenge to the WGBH team.

Zoom brand extensions

Zoomers

Zoomerang

ZoomNooz

Zoomzones

Zoomphenom

CafeZoom

ZoomNoodle

1998

1978

WGBH mission

WGBH enriches people's lives through programs and services that educate, inspire, and entertain, fostering citizenship and culture, the joy of learning, and the power of diverse perspectives.

Zoom lyrics (excerpts)

We're all plugged into one world now
So let's talk
We want to hear from you
Come on, give it a try
And if you like what you see
Turn off your TV
And do it!

Come on and zoom
Yeaahhhh
Come on and zoom
Oooohh
Come on and
zoom zoom zooma zoom

Zoom first aired in the 1970s with the same call to kids: "Turn off the TV and do it!" The program's secondary goal has always been to stimulate an interest in science, math, and engineering. In 1998, WGBH decided to reinvent the series for a new interactive generation. The *Zoom* name and song were so bold and memorable that there was no question but to build on this instantly recognizable brand. One can't say *Zoom* to someone who was around in the '70s without hearing that person spontaneously burst into song, "Come on and zoom zoom zooma zoom."

As the producers began to shape the idea for the new series, Chris Pullman, WGBH vice president of design, put together an internal multidisciplinary design and technology team that would be responsible for *Zoom's* new look and feel. Their goals were to design an updated visual identity and visual language, create a compelling interface and website, and design sets for the TV show, costumes, printed materials, and outreach guidelines for local PBS stations and community groups.

Before design began, the team researched children's television programming and kids' brands in general. The team designed multiple approaches for *Zoom's* brandmark and tested them at schools, where they explained the series and showed the students various solutions. "Although there were approaches that we preferred, they were always voted down by the kids. The designs that our team thought were friendly and kidlike were always considered by the kids to be too young," said Elles Gianocostas, senior designer.

Zoomers on the TV set

The producers went with the kids' choice. The final design, which has inherent movement and an interesting shape, has yellow and orange stripes that are a visual connection to the 1970s logo. The design team developed an exuberant palette of six colors and four patterns that use all the possible color combinations. The set design and the website build on this system of decorative elements. The system was then applied to books, teacher's guides, newsletters, CD-ROMs, stickers, T-shirts, pencils, buttons, scenic design pieces, and games. Over a thousand partner sites use *Zoom* materials, including public TV stations, museums, after-school programs, and libraries.

30 percent of the content is science-based, and the National Science Foundation is a primary funder.

"The original idea for *Zoom* was to create a mythical space for kids. It is kids' voices and ideas that shape *Zoom,* and there is a direct correlation with what one sees on the show and what one does on the web. *Zoom* represents a shift in convergence thinking, in that the website drives broadcast content, when it's usually the other way around," said Meredith Nierman, producer, WGBH Interactive. Ideas that are generated by kids all go into a large database—the interactive team mines it constantly for new web postings, while the television folks look for new content for the show.

"We revisit what *Zoom* is and push it all the time. The way *Zoom* feels is constantly evolving—both on TV and the web. Each day, we get feedback from the kids about what is or isn't cool, and we can make things happen very quickly. Kids are fascinated with media and TV production, and love seeing their name in lights," said Nierman. "*Zoom* is like effective parenting—we give kids the opportunity to be free and to grow, within an environment that is safe and monitored. After September 11, we have started dealing more directly with some hard things in life."

Zoom was able to build on existing brand equity. The core idea, "By kids, for kids," still works twenty five years later. The idea of interactivity was always part of the vision. Feedback via snail mail has evolved into e-mail. And everything *Zoom* does is an expression based on implicit respect for the kids. When a child sends in any idea, she immediately receives a thank-you PDF with a "Zoomerang" that can be printed and assembled. On top of delivering the *Zoom* brand promise, WGBH has also created a dramatic and measurable change in viewers' science process skills and understanding. Talk about value added!

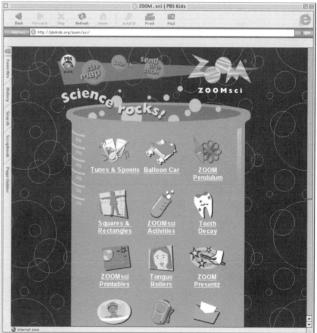

"Mobil has dedicated considerable resources over the past 20 years to the development and maintenance of a strong corporate identity program. Through the efforts of many Mobil people, a readily recognizable image has been established that is representative of our high quality products and services, as well as portraying the company as a profitable, progressive, and environmentally sensitive business enterprise," said Allen E. Murray, CEO, Mobil Corporation, in the *Mobil Graphic Standards Manual.* "I know that I can count on all Mobil personnel to share this commitment to design excellence by following this manual carefully." These strong statements reveal not only insightful leadership, but the kind of top-down commitment necessary to leverage identity as a growth strategy.

How did Mobil, a global company with a presence in over a hundred countries, arrive at this strategy? The mid-sixties in America were characterized by the growth of the suburbs. In many of the new suburban developments, gas stations were simply being zoned out of the neighborhood. Rawleigh Warner Jr., the man who ultimately became the chairman of Mobil realized that if Mobil could make its gas stations appropriate and acceptable in these developments, it would represent a significant opportunity. Warner hired Eliot Noyes, an architectural and industrial design consultant, on the strength of the work he had done for IBM. Noyes implemented a unified design strategy that encompassed everything from product design through advertising and architecture. Noyes, who had worked with Paul Rand on IBM, decided to collaborate with Chermayeff & Geismar, and the rest became design history. It was 1965.

"The problems that needed solving were not at all mysterious, and very clear to see," said Tom Geismar, principal. "While doing our best to understand all of the issues involved, in the end you need to produce a visual mark. We don't call ourselves image or brand consultants—we have chosen to stake a claim in the area of design and being able to come up with creative, intelligent and lasting solutions."

1933

1911

1955

1933

1965

1955

1911

1965

1925

Mobil's name, trademarks, and colors had evolved over a series of mergers for more than one hundred years. In 1965, the existing identity had numerous elements. The Pegasus has been around in various forms since the early twentieth century, and the colors, red and blue, had a lot of brand equity for the company. Geismar's vision was to dramatically simplify the trademark and create a unified visual language for the company. In the customized alphabet, the distinctive red *o*'s are always perfect circles. The circle theme even carried through to Noyes' design for radically new service stations with round canopies and cylindrical pumps. Everything Geismar designed had a monumental simplicity, which stood apart from the clutter of the American landscape. Chermayeff & Geismar also simplified and standardized the language across product lines. No detail was overlooked.

Noyes and Geismar made the first presentation together—they showed the entire unified program from the station design, the pump, the alphabet, the packaging, advertising, and, of course, the trademark. It was approved by an enlightened management team that understood the far-reaching benefits and was willing to make the necessary investment of capital.

By 1966, the name Mobil had become so well known that the corporate name was changed from Socony Mobil Oil Company to the Mobil Oil Corporation. Unlike their competitors, the Mobil service stations always looked clean and well organized. Even a container of motor oil was an opportunity to position the company as advanced, established, and streamlined. Throughout the program, color is used purposefully— from the refineries through the retail shelf space, everything was designed to be logical and achieve the desired perception. The system is based on the philosophy

that the primary messages should always be emphasized with bright colors to attract attention, while the balance of color should appear in a neutral environment. Geismar designed two versions of the trademark. The smart one-color version uses concentric circles to replace the red *o* to convey the same intention.

"Over the next thirty years, we were Mobil's design consultants," said Geismar. "We've worked with three chairmen who cared about design and believed that it was important to the future success of the organization." A management structure to support this strategy was developed and communicated in the *Mobil Graphic Standards Manuals.*

The standards that Chermayeff & Geismar created anticipated every possible scenario in order to control quality and to protect Mobil's investment in this global initiative. "Ideally you would have considerable flexibility, but to do that in a very large global organization is very difficult," Geismar said. Over the years, the standards evolved into new streamlined formats to reflect changing technology and marketing strategies.

After Mobil's merger with Exxon, Chermayeff & Geismar's long-standing relationship with Mobil ended. But one of the most recognizable trademarks in the world endures. It continues to be sustainable, differentiated, and unique.

After all these years, trademarks still engage my senses. Why and how they work is mysterious. To simplify ideas and to make them clear, for me, is one of life's greatest joys. I believe that if you ask people what they think are the best trademarks out there, they will invariably tell you about an organization that is doing very well. The marks take on the attributes of the organization and they merge. The marks become global reminders that stimulate recall.

Tom Geismar, Chermayeff & Geismar

Household mail response rates to the U.S. Census, conducted every ten years, had fallen from 78 percent in 1970 to 65 percent in 1990. If the trend continued, the forecast projected that forty six million residences would need to be counted by door-to-door enumeration—a huge taxpayer expense. "Go to Madison Avenue and get someone to figure this out," was the mandate given by Congress to Census Bureau Director Martha Farnsworth Riche. "In order to boost response rates, you need someone who understands branding, identity, and information design," advised Sylvia Harris, creative director at Two Twelve Associates. "Then you need a marketing and advertising plan."

Over one hundred million households need to open up the census form by a certain day. Within a week, they have to fill it out and get it out to their mailbox. How do you make 118 million people do what you want? "First thing that you have to do is ask them," said Harris. "You ask them like you would ask your children. You make your expectations clear with firmness and kindness. If you don't ask them, they won't do it. In the past nobody asked them. No one marketed the Census—it was assumed that people would do it because of their patriotic duty."

Every decade, the U.S. government conducts a census. The results affect how taxpayer money is spent and are used to determine which communities will receive federal program funds.

"You need to get people's attention," said Harris. "To do that requires marketing—the same kind of effort that a consumer products company would put in because you're competing with everything from junk mail to TV and radio." Two Twelve's preliminary audit examined the history of the Census Bureau, along with that of other government institutions. They went to the Ad Council's archives to look at successful national campaigns such as Smokey the Bear and the seat belt campaign.

Harris created a five-point strategy that was approved by the director. All subsequent presentations were made to the forty-person Steering Committee. "I'm very process-oriented, and if you have everyone involved from the start, you don't have any naysayers that can derail the process," said Harris. "It's better to get all the stuff

out on the table early—ultimately, it's more efficient." The process was also made easier by a strong and forward-thinking director, who was involved at each key decision point.

"You're building a brand. Every household in America has to recognize it." In the past, the Census Bureau had used symbols. User testing confirmed what Two Twelve recognized early on—they needed a wordmark to say clearly, directly, and immediately what it was—not a mascot or a symbol. An independent research firm tested the brand identity, and subsequently Two Twelve designed guidelines for a unified approach for all census communications.

Two Twelve's information design approach was about accessibility, clarity, and understanding and was completely user-centered. "We viewed the census form as an information product that has a lot of human interaction. You need to show design solutions to real people because your assumptions about what might work just might be off track," said Harris. Everything from visual acuity to type size, color, and navigational cues was analyzed and tested in their process. In addition, the team received research findings from a direct mail specialist.

"In the past, the census had never told people why they should respond. Our recommendation was to market the benefits and to be more marketing-focused," said Harris. Two Twelve developed a comprehensive advertising plan. Boutique firms that represented each ethnic group were retained, and in the end, Young & Rubicam was hired to launch the national campaign. Bottom line: the declining trend was halted, although the final results have yet to come in.

Five-point strategy

1 Develop a brand identity for the 2000 census that is consistently applied in all communications.

2 Vigorously market the benefits the census brings to citizens.

3 Design forms that would fit the content, support data processing requirements, use intuitive navigational aids, look simple and fast to complete, and use the visual language of contemporary communications.

4 Borrow user testing models from the product design community to allow the public to co-design the final product.

5 Establish a steering committee with members from every group that had a stake in the outcome.

"We want to build one of the world's great brands by building an organization devoted to revolutionizing the world's relationship with energy," said Lord Browne, CEO of BP. Browne believes that "in a global marketplace, branding is crucial in attracting customers and business. It is not just a matter of a few gas stations or the logo on pole signs. It is about the identity of the company and the values that underpin everything that you do and every relationship that you have."

The 1998 merger of BP and Amoco created one of the world's largest oil and petrochemical groups. Landor Associates was retained to develop a brand identity that would help unite BP Amoco's employees from two merged companies and signal to the world that this was a new strong global brand. Landor began by reviewing BP Amoco's existing research and conducting new research on the equity of the existing brands.

Landor used a rigorous process to affirm what makes the brand unique, compelling, and differentiated. This included one-on-one interviews with senior managers and culminated in an offsite workshop called Brand Driver. "It's a process that gets management under the skin of the brand," says Andrew Welch, client director, Landor Associates. During this workshop, senior managers and marketing executives worked collaboratively to substantiate the core values and attributes of the new brand. It led to the affirmation of the already emerging values (performance, innovation, green, and progressive) and a commitment to transform the organization and transcend the sector.

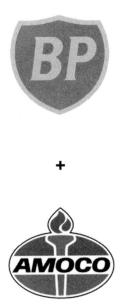

Landor developed a brief that distilled BP's brand essence for their creative team. After assessing the strengths and weaknesses of numerous naming options, Landor made a strong recommendation to retain the BP name, based on its significant equity, high-quality perception, and global heritage. The theme 'Beyond Petroleum', developed by Ogilvy & Mather, was recommended as a central concept to unify all actions, behaviors, and communications for the BP brand. It signaled a BP imperative to go beyond conventional ways of thinking and doing. "We need to reinvent the energy business; to go beyond petroleum. Not by abandoning oil and gas—but by improving the ways in which it is used and produced so that our business is aligned with the long term needs of the world," said Lord Browne.

Landor designed a series of marks, identities, and 'look and feels.' The CEO and senior management chose the helios strategy, which tested strongly against the qualities of progressive, forward-thinking, innovative and, environmental. Although there were safer choices, Browne's unshakeable commitment to the vision meant he was willing to take the risk. "Ultimately the choice that he made was audacious," said Welch. The reaction was swift; it sparked both positive associations and negative reactions. The helios trademark shifted the paradigm of what the petroleum industry should look and feel like.

Building a great brand requires a commitment to align a company's business with its external expressions and its internal culture. Key to the new strategy was ensuring that a hundred thousand employees in a hundred countries understood how to align their actions with BP's core values. "Branding is not about checking the box and moving on. Brands are living, and breathing—they need to be embraced, monitored, and adapted," says Welch. Landor developed a series of employee workshops and exercises to engage employees in the new vision, and engender discussions about ways to live the brand in their daily lives. The Brand Centre, an online resource for guidelines, demonstrates how the brand is used throughout BP and helps each employee play a part in building the brand.

"We believe that branding is a journey and not a destination," said Welch. BP's ongoing commitment to building the brand involves annual surveys to monitor the brand's impact externally on business performance, and relations with consumers and communities, and internally on brand perception, employee morale and job satisfaction. BP's desire to translate the brand into action has had visible results aligning behavior, activities, and communications.

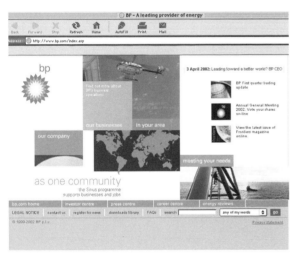

Cingular Wireless, a joint venture between Bell South Mobility and SBC Wireless, was launched in September 2000. Representing the largest consolidation of brands in the history of the wireless industry, the new name would represent eleven former brands and over twenty one million customers. The new company would become the second largest wireless company in the United States and compete with established brands such as AT&T, Sprint, and Nextel, and recently launched brands such as Verizon Wireless and VoiceStream.

"Our greatest challenge was developing a compelling, credible, and instantly familiar name in a six-week time frame," said Jamie Koval, principal of VSA Partners. "Cingular was a late entry into a crowded marketplace and needed to immediately establish itself as a leader. The company was looking for a breakthrough presence."

In order to streamline the process, VSA Partners worked closely with a small communications team made up of members from both companies and led by the company's CEO, Stephen Carter. Once this team became comfortable with the overall brand strategy, name, and identity, a final presentation was made to CEOs of both parent companies.

All of Cingular's competitors were positioning themselves around the expected areas of "access" and "technology." As a result, wireless companies were indistinguishable from one another and faced increased consumer skepticism. In addition, Cingular, in the short term, was not planning to offer anything new in terms of technology or products and services, which meant that the company had to reinforce its position solely through its unique brand essence, name, and identity.

Due to the tight time frame, VSA's research was limited to an extensive, global secondary audit of leading competitors. They also studied category-defining companies, both inside and outside of the telecommunications sector, that were able to build and maintain strong, compelling brands. "We began to realize that the wireless space was evolving from a features-and-functions buying decision to a lifestyle choice," said Koval.

VSA's brand strategy was to position Cingular as the embodiment of human expression. Cingular would allow users to "make their mark" by providing intuitive solutions to all wireless wants and needs. From this strategy, VSA Partners developed a name that was based on a real word with a real meaning—a name that was dramatically differentiated and reflected the new company's goal of becoming the single source for all wireless needs. The naming portion of the project was particularly challenging because linguistic criteria were extremely specific (for instance, the name could not start with *v, s, a, or n*) and the domain name had to be available worldwide.

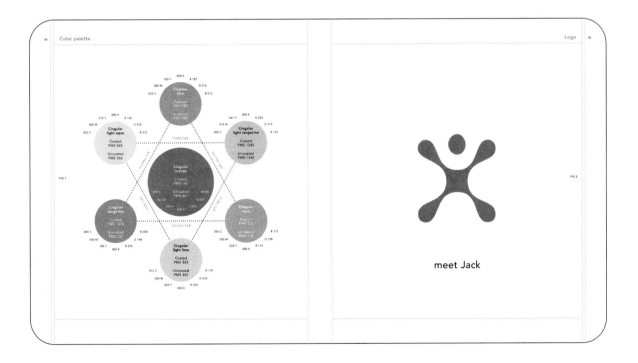

meet Jack

During the naming process, VSA conducted "disaster-check" focus groups in five U.S. markets with a short list culled from thousands of names. The research was specifically designed to uncover negative associations with any of the names in twelve languages. This research was never intended to help select the final name recommendation, but it screened out potential conflicts. Koval pointed out that it's difficult for any organization to embrace a new name. In the case of Cingular, neither CEO of the brand's parent companies immediately warmed to the new name when it was originally presented. "What they ultimately found convincing was when we presented the full potential of the brand, so that it wasn't just a word on a piece of paper," he said. As part of their final identity presentation, VSA demonstrated how the flexible identity system could be applied in different media. Their examples included packaging, literature, advertisements, retail environments, merchandise, and a stationery system.

The Cingular logo was designed to directly reinforce the idea of human expression and the goal of helping users "make their mark." The brandmark, known internally as "Jack," stands for the pinnacle of individuality and freedom of expression. "We wanted a mark that would celebrate individuality and self-expression in a category dominated by sameness," said Koval. "The mark was purposely designed to be both

VSA Partners believes that the Cingular program was ultimately successful because it followed the firm's core principles for the project:

The client's desire to achieve a true breakthrough brand

The strategic soundness of a core brand essence and positioning

The appropriateness of an emotional approach to the identity

Consistent access to and support from senior leadership

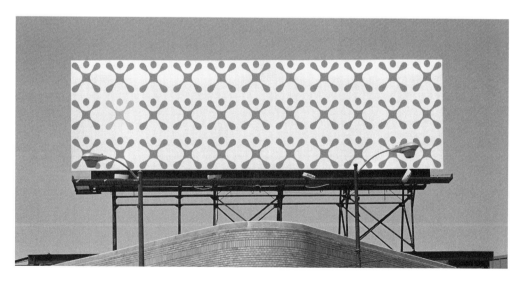

a static and dynamic element—print and electronic. We wanted the overall identity program to feel warm, approachable and simple." This principle drew VSA's designers to basic round forms, straightforward typography, and brightness. The choice of orange as the corporate color was based on the audit of the competitive set and the desire to put some visual distance between Cingular and its peers.

Once the name and identity were approved, they were presented to Cingular's signage provider and national advertising agency. This step has ensured that the Cingular brand has been communicated a manner consistent with its original intent. While VSA typically implements and launches its brand identity programs, its role in the Cingular brand was specific to positioning, naming, and identity. Backed by a $300 million media campaign, the Cingular brand was brought to life, making it an instantly recognizable icon. "It was exhilarating to create the foundation of something so visible and valuable," said Koval, "and to see how it's become imbedded in our culture."

In 1998, two corporate behemoths merged to form the biggest bank in the world. The Travelers Group, with the famous red umbrella, bought Citicorp, the company with the italic caps and a compass rose designed by Dan Friedman. The merger, which combined these two financial institutions literally under one umbrella, spanned 102 countries, 270,000 employees, 190 million customers, and more than $89 billion in assets.

 The merging companies retained Michael Wolff, a British brand strategist, to develop a unified and compelling brand strategy for the future. For the identity creation phase, Wolff recommended Pentagram partner Michael Bierut to the new entity's global brand manager. Bierut brought in Paula Scher. He managed the project and Scher led the design team. Scher quickly realized the lowercase *t* in "Citi" could be envisioned as an umbrella handle. When she put the familiar red arc over it, the *t,* which also stood for Travelers, became the perfect symbol of the merged entity.

Mergers can be highly political. Powerful CEOs will frequently use their logos as chess pieces in an extended match. Finding a way to maintain the equity of both brands would be central to the new identity's success, given that the merging

Paula Scher's first sketch

citi
citicredit
citisalomon
citiSSB
eciti
citif/i
citigold
citiselect
citifuture
citiphone

companies each had highly visible brands and dissimilar corporate cultures. Although Pentagram made the commitment to deliver a logo in ten weeks, the new identity did not accompany the press announcement, as originally planned. What actually transpired was a two-year process of incremental changes.

What was the compelling brand strategy? "We want to become the bank of the future. We really need to imagine talking to our two billionth customer," said Michael Wolff. "She is an eleven-year-old girl named Melissa. She thinks of banking services in a whole new way, grows up doing all of her banking on line, and expects everything to be simple. She lives in the world of McDonald's, Nike, the Gap, and Coke." Wolff and the Pentagram team wanted to reduce the brand name to "Citi." Showing this new vision in a field of the world's super brands made a memorable impression and accelerated the acceptance of the unified strategy.

Pentagram confirmed the validity of its recommended solution through extensive testing against other concepts and created a logical brand architecture. The elegant solution used "Citi" as the core prefix, which could then accommodate an infinite list of suffix services and products. Secondary visual language and numerous

Citi in a field of superbrands.

applications were designed to demonstrate the personality and flexibility of the program. Originally envisioned as a red and black program, it became more important to use the blue from Citicorp and the Traveler's red. The "blue wave," a core element of Citibank's brand equity, was reconceived into a gradation dubbed "the next wave."

But developing a compelling brand strategy and a world-class identity is only half the job. Developing what Scher calls "the prevailing logic" was pivotal. In addition to getting buy-in from the CEOs, slowly moving it through the complex web of senior managers was a painstaking and necessary job.

Rather than creating a three-hundred-page identity manual, Pentagram created a "thought book" in which the essence of the brand identity is communicated in a way that can be used both internally and externally with advertising agencies and design firms. When Fallon Worldwide was selected to create a global advertising strategy, the company met with Pentagram to understand the origin and spirit of the program.

Final design, credit card

After Sandy Weill became the prevailing CEO, Fallon Worldwide launched an imaginative advertising campaign, and the organization began to adopt the new identity. From new shimmering credit cards in consumer's wallets to giant billboards on Times Square, the Citi signage is a visible addition to the streetscape. Lippincott & Margulies was retained by Citi to plan and implement global signage applications.

"These achievements would not have been possible without the judicious support of Citi's global brand manager and global advertising manager," said Scher. "These brand champions kept the organization focused on the brand track throughout the long, circuitous process."

The vision of reducing the brand name to Citi is slowly evolving into a reality. Merged under one umbrella, the two companies have become one.

In December 1999, Pharmacia & Upjohn and the Monsanto Corporation, including its G. D. Searle unit, announced a merger that would create a powerful new competitor in the global pharmaceutical industry. This was only four years after Pharmacia AB and The Upjohn Company had merged. By late January 2000, the transition team had selected Pharmacia Corporation as the name of the merged entity because it captured the strong pharmaceutical heritage of both companies. Monsanto would retain its name and operate as an autonomous global agricultural subsidiary.

Pharmacia has research, sales, and manufacturing operations in more than sixty countries, and has over fifty-nine thousand employees. It is known to have one of the strongest global sales forces in the industry, with over ten thousand sales professionals.

In the spirit of the merger, management combined the Pharmacia name with Searle's proprietary blue color and distinctive typeface design. Crosby Associates, who had designed Searle's identity program, was retained to build the branding program and global visual identity system. Crosby came to the table with an understanding of the pharmaceutical industry and extensive experience working with extremely complex organizations.

Pharmacia's new logotype, designed by Landor Associates, was inspired by Searle's unique "alpha A" typography. Temporary standards for stationery and signing were quickly developed. The next priority was to develop brand architecture and policy recommendations. Guidelines for the names and logotypes for the numerous brand and legal names, subsidiaries, joint ventures, franchises (areas of expertise), sales organizations, and products needed to be aligned. Crosby began the complex process of analyzing all of the names, visual identifiers, environments, and applications, and their interrelationship and impact upon one another.

 Pharmacia &Upjohn + *SEARLE* =

PHARMACIA

"Our goal was to organize all the names that were used throughout the corporation into meaningful, understandable and leverageable categories, and to establish guidelines that govern how and where each name is used. We needed to ensure that all the names and visual identifiers were compatible within the culture of the organization and to build the Pharmacia brand," said Bart Crosby, principal. Crosby Associates gathered information regarding Pharmacia's strategic direction and imperatives, business environment, customer perception studies, and interim brand positioning. They also reviewed Pharmacia & Upjohn's previous positioning documents and conducted extensive interviews of senior management.

Crosby recommended unifying all parts and products under the Pharmacia name with a dynamic system that would create greater awareness among customers, shareholders, regulatory, and employee audiences. However, the most challenging aspect was to develop a strategy that would support future expansion of new sales forces. The legacy names—Searle, Upjohn, Pharmacia & Upjohn—had "door opening power" and equity that was substantial. "We needed to develop a system that would maintain or invent a range of selling unit names that would continue to increase the frequency of sales calls to core customers—specifically general-practitioner physicians and clinicians," said Crosby.

Five alternative systems explored varying degrees of prominence of the parent, examined the interrelationship of Pharmacia to the legacy names and existing visual identities, and considered new naming strategies for individual sales forces.

Pharmacia Sales Force Business Card System   alternative **A**

PHARMACIA

Joe Smith
Vice President
Global Compensation & Benefits

Pharmacia Corporation
100 Route 206 North
Peapack, New Jersey 07977
t 555.123.4567 f 555.123.4568
www.pharmacia.com
joe.smith@pharmacia.com

This system:
• Retains names and logotypes of the legacy sales organizations.
• Expands the number of sales forces by "inventing" new names.
• Uses a minimal size "a Pharmacia company" tagline to indicate ownership.

Comments:
Using legacy names and logotypes produces a substantially different visual and verbal presentation for each of the sales forces. However, this approach will produce minimal recognition for Pharmacia, and does not support the building of a corporate brand or reputation.
The products detailed by the individual sales representative may be listed on either the front or the back of the card.

SEARLE
a PHARMACIA company

Anne Jones
Sales Representative

Celebrex   100 Route 206 North
Ambien   Peapack, New Jersey 07977
Daypro   t 555.123.4567 f 555.123.4568
Cytotec   www.pharmacia.com
               anne.jones@pharmacia.com

Pharmacia & Upjohn
a PHARMACIA company

Anne Jones
Sales Representative

Celebrex   100 Route 206 North
Ambien   Peapack, New Jersey 07977
Daypro   t 555.123.4567 f 555.123.4568
Cytotec   www.pharmacia.com
               anne.jones@pharmacia.com

Upjohn
a PHARMACIA company

Anne Jones
Sales Representative

Xanax   100 Route 206 North
Medrol   Peapack, New Jersey 07977
Caverject   t 555.123.4567 f 555.123.4568
Detacin   www.pharmacia.com
               anne.jones@pharmacia.com

Hypothia
a PHARMACIA company

Anne Jones
Sales Representative

Xanax   100 Route 206 North
Medrol   Peapack, New Jersey 07977
Caverject   t 555.123.4567 f 555.123.4568
Detacin   www.pharmacia.com
               anne.jones@pharmacia.com

Physicia
a PHARMACIA company

Anne Jones
Sales Representative

Celebrex   100 Route 206 North
Ambien   Peapack, New Jersey 07977
Daypro   t 555.123.4567 f 555.123.4568
Cytotec   www.pharmacia.com
               anne.jones@pharmacia.com

Inventia
a PHARMACIA company

Anne Jones
Sales Representative

Xanax   100 Route 206 North
Medrol   Peapack, New Jersey 07977
Caverject   t 555.123.4567 f 555.123.4568
Detacin   www.pharmacia.com
               anne.jones@pharmacia.com

Pharmacia Sales Force Business Card System   alternative **C**

PHARMACIA

Joe Smith
Vice President
Global Compensation & Benefits

Pharmacia Corporation
100 Route 206 North
Peapack, New Jersey 07977
t 555.123.4567 f 555.123.4568
www.pharmacia.com
joe.smith@pharmacia.com

This system:
• Retains and displays the legacy sales organization names combined with sequential, differentiating suffixes.
• Expands the number of sales forces by adding more suffixes to each of the legacy names.
• Creates a visual format that allows the Pharmacia logotype to act as an endorsement.

Comments:
The legacy names are dominant and are coupled with fairly neutral suffixes in order to produce "waves" of selling—similar sales force names, but each detailing a separate set of products.
The products detailed by the individual sales representative are listed on the card.

SearleAlpha

Anne Jones
Sales Representative

Celebrex   100 Route 206 North
Ambien   Peapack, New Jersey 07977
Daypro   t 555.123.4567 f 555.123.4568
Cytotec   www.pharmacia.com
               anne.jones@pharmacia.com

PHARMACIA

SearleBeta

Anne Jones
Sales Representative

Celebrex   100 Route 206 North
Ambien   Peapack, New Jersey 07977
Daypro   t 555.123.4567 f 555.123.4568
Cytotec   www.pharmacia.com
               anne.jones@pharmacia.com

PHARMACIA

UpjohnAlpha

Anne Jones
Sales Representative

Xanax   100 Route 206 North
Medrol   Peapack, New Jersey 07977
Caverject   t 555.123.4567 f 555.123.4568
Detacin   www.pharmacia.com
               anne.jones@pharmacia.com

PHARMACIA

UpjohnBeta

Anne Jones
Sales Representative

Xanax   100 Route 206 North
Medrol   Peapack, New Jersey 07977
Caverject   t 555.123.4567 f 555.123.4568
Detacin   www.pharmacia.com
               anne.jones@pharmacia.com

PHARMACIA

PharmaciaBeta

Anne Jones
Sales Representative

Genotropin   100 Route 206 North
Fragmin   Peapack, New Jersey 07977
Ellence   t 555.123.4567 f 555.123.4568
Healon   www.pharmacia.com
               anne.jones@pharmacia.com

PHARMACIA

PharmaciaGamma

Anne Jones
Sales Representative

Genotropin   100 Route 206 North
Fragmin   Peapack, New Jersey 07977
Ellence   t 555.123.4567 f 555.123.4568
Healon   www.pharmacia.com
               anne.jones@pharmacia.com

PHARMACIA

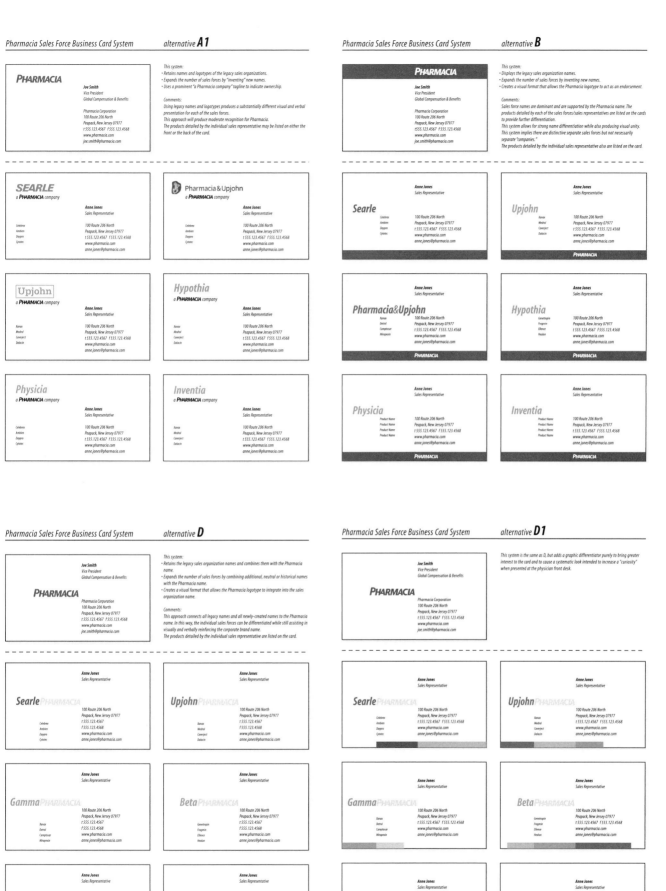

In order to identify the best strategy, a survey was sent to several sales representatives who were advocates for the best interests of both the corporate organization and the various sales forces. Their responses were carefully analyzed. A decision was made to maintain the legacy sales force names, replace their logotypes with a uniform type font and color-code each sales force division. The Pharmacia logo was carried in a narrow blue band at the bottom. Each card also carried the names of the products detailed by the individual reps, printed on the face of the cards.

After the extensive brand architecture issues were resolved, Crosby Associates finalized all identity design and began the massive global implementation of all marketing materials from business forms and stationery through vehicles and signage, promotional literature, trade shows, and presentations. In conjunction with Monigle Associates, an Identity Manager™ website was created and launched in late 2000 that introduced the new branding program. "A highly functional electronic standards evolving manual, it contains virtually all specifications and procedures for the production of all Pharmacia communications and marketing tools," said Crosby.

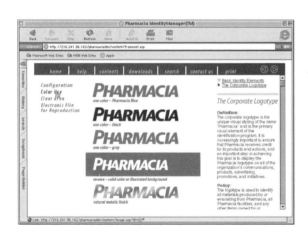

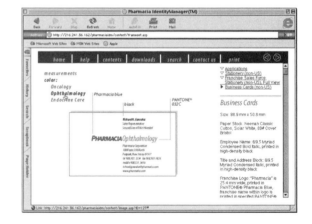

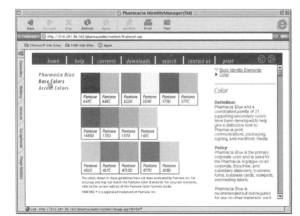

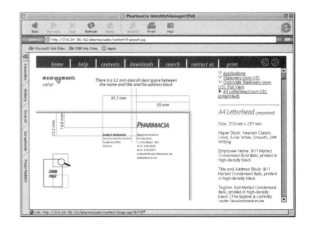

The next significant hurdle was addressing trade dress specifications, which would involve cooperation and input from the marketing, manufacturing, and regulatory departments. An audit was conducted by Crosby, including prior standards developed for Searle and Pharmacia & Upjohn. Crosby developed various trade dress scenarios, which provided the flexibility to accommodate a wide range of products and regulatory needs. Cartons, labels, and blister foil graphics needed to be manufactured in hundreds of configurations and for thousands of items. A plan to phase in new trade dress was begun in mid-2001.

Crosby Associates has an ongoing relationship with Pharmacia to continue developing strategies for building the brand and its distinctive culture. As the new organization takes shape, the role of the brand consultant forms an important bridge between the legacy traditions, procedures, and systems of the prior organizations. Through its responsible and responsive work, Crosby Associates has listened carefully to the needs of the whole organization, including marketing, sales, advertising, regulatory, business services, manufacturing, and facilities.

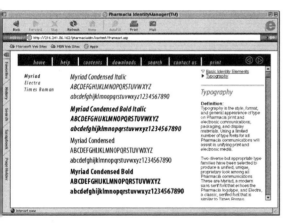

In conjunction with Monigle Associates, an Identity Manager™ website was created to introduce the new branding program.

"In 1998, we became America's bank. We became the new Bank of America," said Hugh McColl Jr., chairman and CEO in his annual report. Two robust healthy financial services companies joined together to take advantage of scale, increased product offerings, and the deregulation of the financial services industry. NationsBank, a forty two-year-old U.S. bank headquartered in the South, merged with Bank of America, a national institution founded in 1905. The combined corporation presently has 143,000 employees and has financial centers in forty eight states, the District of Columbia, and thirty eight countries.

Enterprise IG was given one hundred days to conduct research, develop a positioning strategy, recommend a brand name, design a brand identity, and plan a launch. "We needed to answer basic branding questions: What ideas, traits and benefits would drive the new brand? What would the merging of businesses and cultures mean to customers around the globe? What powerful, lasting impression would the bank's leadership want the new brand to make?" said Bob Loughhead, VP, Enterprise IG (formerly senior VP at Bank of America).

Audit brainstorming wall
at Enterprise IG

Enterprise IG oversaw five thousand interviews on four continents with individuals in twenty-one customer segments. Intensive person-to-person interviews were conducted with the new integrated leadership. At the same time, the brand team was beginning to map out competitor strengths, assess the image of the merged banks, explore every possible naming option, and develop trial positioning statements.

One of the largest challenges was to build agreement on the new brand name. Which name would have the greatest long-term value? Decision making in mergers is often difficult, and made more so by the pressure of time. Enterprise IG had developed a data-driven objective model, named Brand Analytics, to test various positioning strategies and names and to eliminate personal and political bias from decision making.

The new positioning strategy Enterprise IG developed echoed the bold and visionary style of the new chairman and CEO: "We have the courage, passion, and means to make banking work for you in ways it never has before." The name, however, was not finalized until the conclusion of the project. The team's intuition was supported by the new data, and the Bank of America name was recommended as a "declaration of leadership in commerce and finance."

The design team, with knowledge of the research and positioning strategy, only had six weeks to develop and finalize the brand identity system. The brand identity had to appeal to many segments from the local community to the affluent investor to the global institutional investor. The design team collected hundreds of American symbols and images as part of their audit. They needed to consider an enormous range of applications, from automatic teller machines and building signage to stock certificates and business cards.

"The final design is a symbol of the American landscape—woven, flexible, and suggesting security and movement" says Helen Keyes, Managing Director, Creative. An overall visual system was designed with a unified curved grid that organized the brand content, regardless of the medium. Red, white, and blue are used consistently for the most visible consumer-based communications, with an additional system of colors and images appropriate for different segments.

Enterprise IG presented the new brand and positioning strategy, messaging, brand name, and brand identity system to the CEO and his business heads. They approved the entire program in a two-hour session. Enterprise IG attributes the swiftness of the decision making to the rigor of their process.

The project launch was realized worldwide in one day and announced through printed materials, electronic communications, and advertising. Coordination of printers, writers, signage fabricators, and merchandise manufacturers was necessary. The project was kept highly confidential until the launch date.

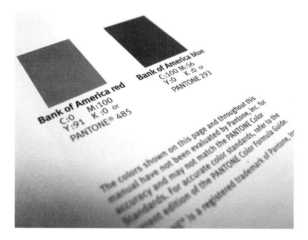

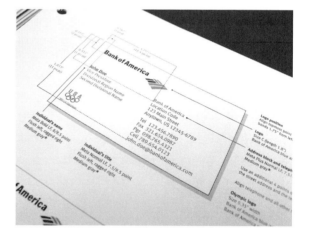

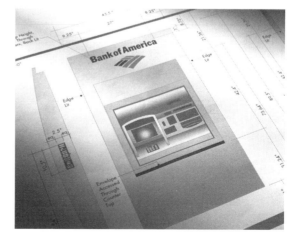

Bank of America's standards and guidelines manual

"We hired Frankfurt Balkind to build awareness of our new technology and to drive sales leads," said Diane Fraiman, Sanctum's vice president of marketing. As the leader in an emerging field, start-up Sanctum had developed new technology to protect websites from hackers. The company's software addresses the fifth level of vulnerability—the website itself, behind authentication, viruses, encryption, and firewalls. Hackers exploit bugs in the website to steal credit card, health, and other confidential information, as well as deface the website. Rather than keep out intruders, the software makes whoever touches the site behave correctly. Prior to Sanctum's technology, the target market, Fortune 1000 companies, had to fix holes and bugs in their code manually.

At the time that Frankfurt Balkind was hired, Sanctum was called Perfecto Technologies. Frankfurt Balkind's challenge was to find a more appropriate name and to create a brand strategy, an advertising campaign, collateral materials, and a website to market the company and its products.

Frankfurt Balkind's process began with interviewing six company executives, analyzing the positioning and messages of other web security companies, and speaking with industry analysts, including The Gartner Group. "Providing a ninety-

Sanctum's former name and identity

page deck that extrapolates what our client tells us has little value," said Aubrey Balkind, principal. "We create hypotheses and test their validity against the reality." Frankfurt Balkind positioned Sanctum as the first viable security system for the most vulnerable part of the web. Their first step was to create a core branding concept that would galvanize companies to recognize the need for this level of security. Dubbed "web perversion," the concept dramatized the malicious nature of the problem and brought heat and attention to the vulnerability caused by bugs in the web application itself. Frankfurt Balkind tested the term with both technology analysts and the press, who not only understood it but found their curiosity piqued by the intriguing concept.

In renaming Perfecto Technologies, Frankfurt Balkind strove for a name that would communicate the confidence of feeling secure, rather than the fear of violation. The name, Sanctum, means safe at the core. The brandmark reflected the intention of the name with an all-seeing, intelligent eye providing a "lighthouse" feeling of security. It is accompanied by the tagline "Save your site." "Our goal in creating a brand identity is not surface consistency but inner coherence," Balkind said. The project took twelve weeks from start to delivery of all the materials, including a flexible communications system.

Frankfurt Balkind created the Sanctuminc.com website, which dramatized the four types of perverts: Type A, who steals assets; Type B, who changes merchandise prices; Type C, who steals credit card information; and Type D, who defaces sites. The brochure cleverly simulates how a hacker scans the URL to find holes in the code.

While Sanctum's primary decision maker and brand champion was the vice president of marketing, the CEO and board of directors made the final decisions. "Launching any new company or product has many risks, especially when it is a new field," said Balkind. Two launch events, in New York and San Francisco, were set a week apart. Sanctum issued a bold challenge to hackers to, within the week, break into the SanctumInc.com website that Frankfurt Balkind developed using the technology. No one did.

Two hundred executives and press attended launch events. The launches, produced by special events producer Ellen Michaels, included magicians dressed as businesspeople who surreptitiously "pickpocketed" the guests. At the start of her speech, Sanctum's CEO then returned all the wallets, belts, and jewelry to the unsuspecting audience to dramatize their vulnerability. Within ninety days of the launch, Sanctum's monthly sales had catapulted into the six figures, as the sales force closed thirteen deals with end users and acquired ten new partners. Sanctum received wide and positive press coverage. Web responses showed an average of twenty to twenty five minutes per visit for demos of the product and five to ten minute for information visits, which are above industry averages.

Advertisement

In the marketing cycle we move people from first time awareness to long-term customer relationships.

The goal is to create brand coherence across all media forms without having to impose inhibiting executional rules that freeze the brand in time and conform to the lowest common denominator. That way each medium can be used to its best advantage.

Our application systems focus more on what you can do than on what you can't.

Advertising often is the area where companies spend the most money, and is the quickest and most focused communicator of a brand.

There is a lot of confusion about the meaning of "brand" and "identity." A brand is the essence of the company or a product. It manifests itself in many ways— from the type of employees and the way they behave and talk to the identity and how messages are expressed in advertising, direct mail, web site, collateral, office space, product, etc. Identity, on the other hand, is a long-term expression of the brand and more ambiguous strategically to allow for change and growth.

The executional trigger of a coherent strategy is resonance. It works best when the audience incorporates the messages into their work or personal lives.

You can create an identity, build a website, launch an ad campaign and fail to create a brand.

Aubrey Balkind,
CEO, Frankfurt Balkind

201

When the line of Tazo teas appeared on shelves in 1995, its strikingly elegant yet earthy packaging was like a new sensory magnet. The design quickly captured a wider audience. People were buying Tazo simply for the packaging. Why? Because the packaging articulated what was inside.

"People can feel indifferent to a brand despite the excellence of visual imagery if a brand doesn't deliver on its promise," said Steve Sandstrom, Tazo's identity designer and principal of Sandstrom Design in Portland, Oregon. "The beauty of Tazo is that the brand does deliver, inside and out," he says.

The fact that Tazo's success came during an explosion of new tea products is a tribute to Tazo's co-founders' understanding of brand differentiation and niche marketing, although it is unlikely they would use those terms. Steve Smith, an acknowledged "tea master," and his business partner, Steve Lee, were more focused on getting the public to sample and subscribe to Smith's blend of teas.

Smith and Lee were creative and entrepreneurial, and they were willing to take the risks associated with introducing a new product in a marketplace full of competitors. Many of those bottled tea products, while employing slick and bold marketing strategies, actually contained very little of the real thing—tea! Furthermore, many of the products' ingredients were artificial, even down to the fruit flavorings. Smith believed his concoction of tea, real fruit juice, and herbs would not only appeal to people's taste buds, but also appeal to the consumer looking for a healthy and natural beverage.

But taste alone would not be enough. While tea continues to be the most frequently consumed beverage, aside from water, in most parts of the world, its popularity and perceptions were different in the United States. Tea was an elixir for a winter cold, a quencher for summer thirst, and an alternative for the caffeine-averse. Smith wanted to reintroduce tea to Americans as a beverage unlike any to which they were accustomed.

Smith already had conjured up creative strategies for designing the tea's identity. He had a vision of promoting his tea as a blend that encompasses history and magic, or as Smith said, "Marco Polo meets Merlin." Tea, he said, has ancient, yet somewhat mysterious origins, and its ingredients have the power to soothe, energize, and otherwise affect people's moods.

Smith brought his ideas to Steve Sandoz, a creative director at the advertising agency Wieden & Kennedy. Sandoz then introduced the two to Sandstrom, and the creative process for the brand identity began. Sandoz knew immediately what Smith was trying to create. It wasn't just about a premium product—it was about creating an aura that would make the tea "otherworldly." Needing to find a name to reflect this concept, Sandoz eventually came up with the made-up word "Tazo." The name seemed to be the perfect mix of the Old World—tea being the oldest beverage in the world, aside from water—and the New World—sophisticated and eclectic.

Sandoz presented the name to Sandstrom, who instinctively recognized that evoking tea's ancient origins was the best starting point. Sandstrom did not want to rely on an established typeface—"I was really thinking of hand lettering," he says. So he developed a highly stylized rendering of the Tazo name based on Exocet, an Émigré typeface designed by Jonathan Barnbrook, that featured characters that looked both foreign (but not affiliated with an foreign country) yet recognizable. Sandstrom emphasized the lettering by framing it in a woodcutlike box. He then continued to design what seemed like an entire culture with its own language, artifacts, and storytelling.

At the same time, Sandoz developed a tagline that supported Smith's desire to bring about the rebirth of tea in the United States: "The Reincarnation of Tea." He also avoided using generic and traditional names, opting instead to create names that evoked an emotional connection. He called English Breakfast, a caffeinated black tea, Awake, and an herbal non-caffeinated blend Calm. Other names included Zen, Passion, and Refresh.

The combination of an exceptional product and original visual imagery closed the branding circle. "Quality plus packaging—that's what makes the brand," said Sandstrom. The packaging truly stood out, despite the numerous and established brands—Twinings and Celestial Seasonings among the filtered tea bags, and Snapple among the bottled offerings. The packaging was absolutely different, but not so offbeat or alienating as to arouse suspicion. The packaging exuded good taste, in more ways than one.

Martha Stewart's inimitable style is the soul of Martha Stewart Living Omnimedia, a public company that has made simple beauty and honest design accessible to millions. Unified by a boundless sense of curiosity and a passion for design excellence, a team of experts in food, gardening, craft, decorating, weddings, babies, and kids have transformed the notion of "how to" into a quest for learning and creativity. "There's so much to learn," says Martha Stewart on her TV program, having just interviewed a tea master about the art of infusion and one hundred kinds of tea.

Martha Stewart's vision and a cluster of brand values come alive in a vast and ever-growing range of media and retail channels that span magazines, television, newspapers, in-store, and online catalogs. "Inspiration and information are the heartbeat of the Martha Stewart brand," said Gael Towey, creative director, Martha Stewart Living Omnimedia. "Quality, beauty, originality, and clarity of information are our guiding principles. We adhere to these principles no matter what medium we are in."

Martha Stewart Living was first published in 1990. The magazine was the creative nexus in which design, color, photography, and language created community by telling stories that aroused the senses and created a sense of discovery. The magazine has always functioned as an idea laboratory for the rational and emotional qualities of the brand. The content as well as the visual language are continuously reinvented and recycled to create a consistent experience of the brand. *Martha Stewart: The Catalogue for Living* grew out of hundreds of letters from readers who could not find the tools and ingredients to create the projects they read about in the magazine. The TV programs, which reach over two million viewers each weekday, have the same look and feel, with sets designed by Martha herself.

In the beginning, Doyle Partners collaborated with MSLO to interpret the brand identity for the mass market called Martha Stewart Everyday. Now the packaging and environment is designed exclusively in-house under Towey's direction. The packaging for the extensive product line, indoor signage, and retail environments is both whimsical and intelligent. In every category, packaging is unified by a coherent expression of whiteness and brightness that always allows the product to emerge. "Every time we would crash a new category, we would see how we could exercise the brand and stretch it," said Stephen Doyle, creative director, Doyle Partners. "Our goal has been to make the retail environment exuberant rather than inevitable," says Doyle. As a result, the retail environments have transcended the discount store experience for the customer. In the process, Martha Stewart Everyday has democratized good design at Kmart, which has over 1800 stores.

A commitment to clarity of information is apparent in each expression of the brand in every medium. From the twenty eight varieties of figs that were tested, tasted and photographed for the magazine right down to the instructions on the back of the seed packets and the display of Martha Stewart paint chips at Kmart, the how-to information creates involvement and trust, and is supported by a love of language and legibility.

**Martha Stewart
Living Omnimedia
Brand Values**

Respect our audience.
Never talk down, never design down.
Encourage excellence.
Assume that the audience is sophisticated.
Be active, be curious, be real.
Deliver quality and service at whatever price point.
Glorify the humble, everyday physicality of life.

"Color has been used to create emotion, trigger memory, and give sensation," said Towey, who was the magazine's first art director. "We have always used color as an important ingredient in the magazine's storytelling," she said. Martha's Auracana chickens inspired pastel hues first used in the magazine. From that beginning, a 256-color palette known as Martha Stewart Everyday Colors, a line of interior and exterior paints, was created and became the ninth largest brand, based on sales volume, in the U.S. The color names—Himalayan Eyes, Ursa Minor, Book Binding Green— reflect the brand sensibilities.

Towey brought in a cadre of world-renowned photographers to glorify the beauty of everyday objects—an approach that became intrinsic to the soul of the brand. Under her direction, even a common garden hose takes on a new elegance when it coils around a lush garden. The 456 packets in the line of seeds feature photographs of flowers, herbs, or vegetables held in a hand to give the customer an immediate sense of scale. But the details are pure Martha: the hand grasping the French radish has earth under the nails, whereas the bouquet of sweet peas is held lightly by manicured fingers; succinct guidelines and garden hints are juxtaposed with etymology and botanical literary allusion.

A brand is how a reader, a viewer, a customer, or a listener feels about a product.

Gael Towey

Each new brand extension has been logical and continuous. Publishing innovations have opened up new markets that appeal to consumers at different points in their life cycle. What began as a magazine evolved into thirty two books, four magazines, one syndicated and three cable TV programs, and thousands of products. Bed and bath evolved into kitchen products and paint lines, which evolved into products for the garden and holidays. Because this brand vision intuits the potential for beauty and delight in the most ordinary of items—a can of poison-free insect repellent or a box of kitchen matches, for example—there is literally no end to the possibilities for its continued evolution. "We're going for full sensory assault," says Towey.

Entrepreneurs who start restaurants are usually described as people who do it for love. One of the most volatile business ventures known, statistics show that restaurants are likely to go under in their first year because of high start-up costs, slow business development, and low cash-out value. Even great restaurants don't necessarily survive. Regardless, there is a constant infusion of new restaurants on the streets of New York, where every type of cuisine known to humankind can be found.

Louise Fili specializes in restaurant identities and food packaging. The process always begins with a name, a location, and a dream. "Restauranteurs routinely agonize over the name for months and months. I end up trying to make unpronounceable names pronounceable and dull names exciting." said Fili. She has worked on many projects where the architect is retained before there is a chef and a menu.

One winter afternoon, an experienced business owner and his architect approached Fili with a extremely tight timeline. The restaurant was soon to be opened, and they needed a logo. The restaurant was on Ninety-second Street and named 92 by default. In talking about his vision, the owner said that he wanted it to feel as if the restaurant had always been there. On a recent trip to France, chairs and fixtures had been purchased, and there was some discussion about a classic New York neighborhood experience.

Louise Fili, a food lover and collector of historical identities, is a rare professional who is able to integrate all the interests in her life into her work. From Metrazur, a French bistro at Grand Central Terminal, to Union Pacific, a pan-Asian restaurant, her restaurant experience is extensive.

It ended up being one of the most challenging logos that Fili had ever designed because the numerals 92 were typographically difficult to work with, and there wasn't a clear direction for the restaurant. She went to visit the corner location on the Upper East Side. The 1920s tile floor from the original tenant, Gristede's supermarket, inspired her to consider making the 92 out of hexagonal tiles. Her next action was to ride the subway on both the East and West Sides—"one token," she said proudly—where she took pictures of every mosaic sign that had a nine and a two. She had always been fascinated by the subway signage, since each one is different and created by unknown craftsmen in the early twentieth century.

Inspired by this unlikely intersection of art and wayfinding, Fili designed a full-color logo that simulated the mosaic subway art. Although there is no ninety-second street stop, by the end of her design process she was convinced there was one. Although Fili had designed five other strong logos, she felt passionate about this solution. The owner immediately approved Fili's recommended strategy, since it felt like who he was and what he had imagined.

Fili needed to proceed full speed with the applications. The identity was applied to square double-sided business cards, menus, outdoor awnings, and matches. A children's menu was designed as a placemat, on which the logo is presented in black and white outlined mosaics and given out with red, green, and yellow crayons. It provides a fun experience for children, allowing the parents to focus on adult conversation and a glass of fine wine.

Quality control and time issues are always a challenge in the restaurant business since numerous vendors around the world are used. They each have different technical requirements and require lead times that seem to come out of another century. Matches are always made in Japan and require an eighteen-week lead with a minimum quantity of thirty thousand. Fili usually gets the business card printed first, so that it can be used as an optimum color guide for everyone from the awning painter to the napkin manufacturer.

The restaurant, a successful business venture, looks as if it has always been part of the neighborhood. The business owner paid Fili the highest compliment when he said, "The restaurant never had a direction until we had a logo."

A 92 placemat for children to color

Front of two sided business card

The symbol of the White House Conference on Children is two flowers—one smaller than the other one. One is an adult, perhaps, and the other a child. White papers presented at the conference each used the symbol as a departure point point for an appropriate image. For example, the white paper on handicapped children has a small flower that is missing a leaf, whereas the one on children's rights has an enormous umbrella sheltering two small flowers. Imagination and spontaneity of expression are rarely found in government publications. However, this identity program—designed over thirty years ago, during the Nixon administration—is both playful and intelligent. The conference brought together three thousand teachers from all over the United States to discuss the pressing issues that were affecting the children of the country.

"My first idea was to actually have children do the artwork," said Ivan Chermayeff, principal, Chermayeff & Geismar. "But that idea failed! So I decided to paint the flower symbol with my left hand (even though I am right-handed) as a way of achieving a childlike quality of expression."

During the conference, there were twenty-five white papers that were presented and distributed. Each cover featured a unique interpretation of the subject matter. "This is project could have been stuffy and jargonistic but I thought it was important to find a way of the make it fresh and fun because it was about children," said Chermayeff. He also provided typing grids and character counts for the writers of the white papers, so that the making of all the papers could be accomplished easily, efficiently, and legibly. It worked.

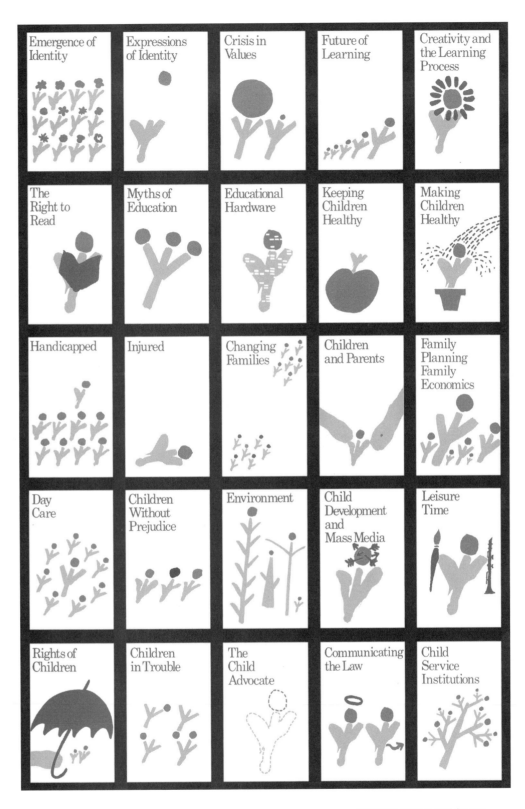

Emergence of Identity	Expressions of Identity	Crisis in Values	Future of Learning	Creativity and the Learning Process
The Right to Read	Myths of Education	Educational Hardware	Keeping Children Healthy	Making Children Healthy
Handicapped	Injured	Changing Families	Children and Parents	Family Planning Family Economics
Day Care	Children Without Prejudice	Environment	Child Development and Mass Media	Leisure Time
Rights of Children	Children in Trouble	The Child Advocate	Communicating the Law	Child Service Institutions

White paper covers used the core
symbol as a departure point for unique
expression.

"Focus on the sidewalks. CCD is about the pedestrian's experience," said Paul Levy, executive director of Philadelphia's Center City District (CCD). Promoting downtown Philadelphia as a thriving urban center is the mission of CCD. Founded in 1990, this private-sector-directed municipal authority helps keep the sidewalks of Center City clean, safe, and attractive and promotes the area as a great place to work, shop, dine, and visit.

In searching for an appropriate symbol for CCD, Joel Katz, principal, Joel Katz Design Associates, knew the symbol should reflect the uniqueness of the downtown area, rather than the city at large. Katz designed a mark based on a diagram of William Penn's original 1681 five-square plan for Philadelphia. Today, these squares function as parks in different neighborhoods of the downtown area. Katz utilized figure-ground ambiguity with the center square. The original northwestern square became a circle in 1919 and gives specificity and identification to an otherwise symmetrical design. The symbol is constructed to place special emphasis on the streetscape and the cohesive structure of the district. The rotated image, which mirrors Philadelphia's actual declination, adds visual interest.

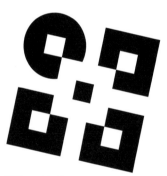

CCD core identity

CCD patch art

The design team presented to the executive director, who championed the symbol through the powerful board, member by member. The biggest hurdle was to overcome the board chairman's expressed preference for a symbolic skyline over what he viewed as an abstract mark. The design team compiled an extensive collection of ads from the Yellow Pages to demonstrate that the city's skyline, which appeared in many company marks, including one for a local escort service, was neither a unique nor appropriate solution.

Uniforms for CCD's two types of on-street employees were the most urgent priority. The first, customer service representatives, function as roving goodwill ambassadors who offer help to visitors and residents, and also act as the eyes and ears of the police. Their uniforms needed a look that was both professional and friendly. Personnel who clean the sidewalks needed to reinforce a positive, service-oriented image. "Authoritative, but not authoritarian. The staff needs to look both official and approachable," said Levy.

The design firm was originally retained to help CCD assemble uniforms from the offerings of local uniform vendors. Instead, Katz persuaded the client to have a major hand in a uniform system that would be highly visible on the urban streetscape. Katz knew it was imperative for the employees to have the credibility of a uniform but not to resemble the police or the parking authority. The uniforms needed to be memorable and upscale and to reinforce a positive image of the city. For the workers, the uniforms needed to foster a sense of pride, responsibility, and esprit de corps.

Katz chose colors designed to be highly visible on a crowded streetscape—colors that were unlike any that usually appear on uniforms. Teal polos for summer and teal parkas in the winter were supplemented by a coordinated system of rain shells, baseball caps, shoulder bags, fanny packs, shirts, pants, and ties. Katz designed a circular embroidered patch in an intense color triad of teal, violet and yellow, with the symbol in the middle that is fabricated in different sizes. In addition, striping is used as an accent on pants, shirts, and parkas. All of the components needed to be produced within severe constraints of time and budget to meet the accelerated schedule for the on-street launch. Extensive clothing vendor research was conducted in order to make the right choices for all the seasonal needs.

The result is a crisp, clean upscale look that is appropriate to CCD's positioning and the safety, security, and maintenance functions. There is both connection and differentiation between the goodwill ambassadors and the maintenance crews. The distinctive uniforms, which have been described as "walking banners," were the most important aspect of the launch. The identity system extended to CCD's vehicles and to all mechanical cleaning equipment with bold and bright decals. Ninety days after the initial launch, the city was enlivened by a comprehensive CCD banner system along Center City's major thoroughfares.

CCD's identity has been applied to newsletters, ad campaigns, the website, brochures, information kiosks, and bus shelter advertising. In addition, Katz designed a Walk/Philadelphia directional signage system for pedestrians that features circular distinctive color-coded maps on signs through the city. CCD's vision for a safer, cleaner, well-managed Philadelphia is realized daily by residents, tourists, and workers. Ten years after the original design, the look and feel of the program continues to be fresh and immediately recognizable.

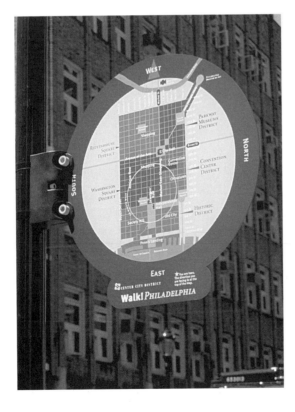

Clemens Family Markets is a family-owned business founded in 1939 that made its niche in home prepared foods and its Pennsylvania Dutch heritage style and quality. Their nineteen supermarkets have a reputation for serving their communities and being family focused. Frequently cited as "supermarket of the year," Clemens continually experiments by adding new amenities to the supermarket experience.

"I have had a vision in my head for years of a food specialty market that would take service to another level," said Jack Clemens, CEO and chairman. "We would offer products that you couldn't get anywhere else—food cooked by chefs on-site that was equal if not better than a food connoisseur would experience at a fine restaurant that you could enjoy in your own home. . . Food sold in an environment that was exceptional, where customers looked forward to shopping there."

When the director of store development saw the large vacant 1930s Chrysler dealership with its big windows and lots of wood and brick, he knew instinctively that this was the space they had been waiting for. The area's average household income, along with a lack of competition, made it a prime retail location.

To make his dream a reality, Clemens put together a core team that included the director of store development, the executive chef, and Bonita Albertson, a designer who specializes in food market environments and identity. Her firm was retained to create an entire brand identity for the new market, including a new name.

Clemens frequently travels around the world to look at food retailers who provide products and experiences that are out of the ordinary. Clemens took his core team on trips to experience what he felt were the best retailers and use the off-site time to brainstorm about what was possible. Albertson introduced the team to looking at retail environments other than food venues—"I wanted our team to think outside of the food world and more about lifestyles. I took them to retailers like Pottery Barn and Crate and Barrel to look at other environments and ways of displaying product."

The team worked closely and collaboratively in open and ongoing discussions for months about the vision, the ambience, the experience, the space, the recipes, and the name. They wanted to build a destination that felt simple, intimate, and friendly and conveyed top-quality food and service.

The interior design evolved first. The wood and brick were sandblasted: "No drywall or soffits. Lots of natural light. . . The essence of the experience needed to focus on the food product—how it is merchandised and how it is presented," said Mark Rohrbach.

After developing numerous names and carefully examining the pros and cons of various strategies, Albertson focused on one name and had one clear vision for the identity. "I wanted to design an identity that was bold and appealing to both genders. We all agreed that the word 'gourmet' was off-putting to inexperienced cooks. The identity had to be differentiated, upscale, and sophisticated. We didn't want to look like an organic food store. I knew that businesses like this grow by word of mouth, and a great-looking shopping bag was like a walking billboard in the suburbs."

The name she developed was Foodsource. The identity features three hand-drawn icons (based on the natural sources of food) juxtaposed to hip typography. The inspiration for the colors, which are asparagus green and terra-cotta, came from a beautiful fall leaf she had collected. The little holes in the leaf were mimicked in the texture of the typography.

Albertson presented an entire brand identity package to the core team. She showed applications carved from Jack Clemens' future dream: uniforms, packaging, shopping bags, signage, and van designs. She even showed how the individual icons could be carved out of planters used on the sidewalk. She walked the team through her process and marketing strategy. The CEO knew as soon as he saw what she had created that this was it.

From the metro wire shelving to the warm, inviting earth tones, the space evolved. As it came close to launch date, Albertson had a lengthy discussion with a Muzak representative. She had a vision for a very eclectic and musically diverse blend of music. Each month a CD with new blended sounds arrives to change the audio atmosphere and compliment the changing food selections. Albertson's final design was the handmade raffia tied announcements that went out to a select group for a private launch party.

Foodsource has been a great success, and a project of passion and pride for the team. The market is in the process of expanding its café space because it is the place to be seen in this small suburban town.

Origins of brand identity

Events that shaped the evolution of brand, design, brand identity, advertising, packaging, and technology

1890: Henry John Heinz markets a line of foods and uses the number *57* as a symbol for his company's variety of products.

1893: Aunt Jemima character is created.

1893: Coca-Cola trademark is registered.

1898: Bibendum, the Michelin Man, is designed.

1898: N. W. Ayer & Son is the first ad agency to create an in-house design department.

1904: Shell Transport and Trading Company (Shell Oil) selects a scallop shell as its trademark.

1911: Morton Salt Girl trademark is introduced.

1911: Procter & Gamble becomes the first company to pay an external agency, J. Walter Thompson, to launch the shortening Crisco.

1916: J. Walter Thompson coins the phrase "It pays to advertise."

1917: BMW logo is designed.

1921: General Mills introduces Betty Crocker in its ad campaigns. Her character becomes the company's trademark in 1947.

1921: J. Walter Thompson hires eminent behavioral psychologist John B. Watson to help with consumer research. He subsequently develops the blindfold testing for advertising.

1930: *Advertising Age* magazine is launched in Chicago.

1931: Brand manager system is developed within Procter & Gamble.

1941: Landor Associates is founded and becomes one of the leading graphic identity firms in the United States.

1949: Bill Bernbach and Ned Doyle establish the advertising agency Doyle Dane Bernbach in New York and devise the concept and creation of "creative teams" that include copywriters and art directors.

1951: CBS "eye" is designed by William Golden.

1954: CBS becomes the largest medium for advertising in the world.

1959: NASA logo is designed by James Modarelli.

Advertising

Branding

1890 → 1910 → 1930 →

Media

Technology

1890 Ty Tolbert Lanston invents the Monotype typesetting machine.

1932 The *Chase & Sanborn Hour* premieres on the radio in a variety/comedy format.

1938 Chester Carlson invents xerography.

1947 *Meet the Press* premieres on NBC's local Washington station and goes network within several weeks.

1948 A poll shows that 68 percent of television viewers remember the names of the programs' sponsors.

1957 *Hidden Persuaders* written by Vance Packard.

BIBLIOGRAPHY

Heller, Steven, and Elinor Pettit. *Graphic Design Time Line: A Century of Design Milestones*. New York: Allworth Press, 2000.

"Graphic Design and Advertising Timeline," *Communication Arts* 41, 1 (1999): 80–95.

1960: International Paper logo designed by Lester Beall.

1961: United Parcel Service (UPS) logo designed by Paul Rand.

1963: American Broadcast Company (ABC) logo designed by Paul Rand.

1964: Mobil Corporation corporate ID program designed by Chermayeff & Geismar.

1965: Exxon oil company logo designed by Raymond Loewy.

1965: Wolff Olins, a British identity firm, is founded in London.

1965: The Pillsbury doughboy trademark is created by Leo Burnett Company.

1967: Levi's logo is designed by Landor and Associates.

1971: Nike swoosh logo is designed by a student, Carol Davidson.

1972: Paul Rand adds stripes to the IBM logotype.

1972: The United Way logo is designed by Saul Bass.

1975: I LOVE NY designed by Milton Glaser.

1975: Thomas J. Watson Jr., president of IBM, delivers the speech "Good Design Is Good Business" at the Wharton School of Business.

1976: Architect and designer Richard Saul Wurman coins "information architecture."

1977: Apple Computer logo is designed by Rob Janoff.

1985: Bass & Associates designs AT&T logo.

1995: TAZO tea line is designed by Sandstrom Design.

2000: BP branded identity launched by Landor Associates.

2001: VSA Partners names Cingular and designs identity.

I love NY: Milton Glaser

1960 → **1970** → **1980** → **1990** **2000** →

1963 Digital Equipment Corporation unveils the first "mini-computer."

1965 International Business Machines (IBM) develops a method for digitally storing type.

1970 The first digitized photographs are introduced.

1971 Intel Corporation develops the microprocessor.

1972 Texas Instruments develops the pocket calculator.

1973 The first fax machines are introduced for commercial use.

1973 The Internet is developed for use by the U.S. Department of Defense.

1977 Apple Computer introduces the Apple II, the first personal computer with color graphics capabilities.

1977 Hewlett-Packard introduces a portable mini-computer.

1980 The compact disc is introduced by Philips Electronics.

1981 Bitstream, the first digital type foundry, is established by Matthew Carter and Mike Parker.

1981 IBM introduces the first personal computer (PC).

1981 Computerized page layout programs are developed.

1982 Apple Computer introduces "Lisa," the first personal computer with a graphical user interface (GUI).

1984 First one-megabyte memory chip is introduced.

1984 Apple Computer unveils the Macintosh, the mouse-driven computer with a graphical user interface.

1985 Adobe Systems introduces PostScript, the programming language that describes the appearance of the printed page.

1986 Adobe Systems releases its drawing program, Illustrator.

1988 The Canon color laser copier is introduced.

1990 Adobe Systems introduces its electronic imaging program, PhotoShop.

1995 Netscape (formerly Mosaic Communications Corporation) goes public.

1995 David Aaker wrote *Building Strong Brands*.

1998 Apple Computer introduces the iMac.

1999 Personal computers are owned by nearly half of all U.S. households.

2001 Tom Peters wrote *Brand You*.

Metric system basics

In the early 1970s, most major countries, with the exception of the United States, adopted the metric system. The metric system is a decimal system of units based on the meter as the international standard unit of length. The meter is approximately equivalent to 39.37 inches. The benefit of the metric system is that it is more convenient and easier to calculate.

Never assume that any U.S. company uses a standard size in their foreign branches until you have researched

U.S. commercial envelopes

	inches	mm
$6^1/4$	$3^1/2 \times 6$	89×152
$6^3/4$	$3^5/8 \times 6^1/2$	92×165
$8^5/8$	$3^5/8 \times 8^5/8$	92×220
7	$3^3/4 \times 6^3/4$	95×171
Monarch ($7^3/4$)	$3^7/8 \times 7^1/2$	98×190
9	$3^7/8 \times 8^7/8$	98×225
10	$4^1/8 \times 9^1/2$	105×241
11	$4^1/2 \times 10^3/8$	114×264
12	$4^3/4 \times 11$	121×279
14	$5 \times 11^1/2$	127×292

U.S. A-style envelopes

A-2	$4^3/8 \times 5^3/4$	111×146
A-6	$4^3/4 \times 6^1/2$	121×165
A-7	$5^1/4 \times 7^1/4$	133×184
A-8	$5^1/2 \times 8^1/8$	140×206
A-long	$3^7/8 \times 8^7/8$	98×225
A-10	$6 \times 9^1/2$	152×241

Conversion formulas

to convert	multiply by
inches to centimeters	2.540
centimeters to inches	.394
inches to millimeters	25.400
millimeters to inches	.039
feet to meters	.305
meters to feet	3.281

Points and picas

12 points = 1 pica
72 points = 1 inch
6 picas = 1 inch

Research compiled by Steff Geisbuhler, Chermayeff & Geismer

Metric business correspondence

Letterhead	210 × 297 mm	8¼ × 11¾″
DL envelope	110 × 220 mm	4⁵/₁₆ × 8⅝″

Business card

Germany Italy Switzerland	85.5 × 54 mm (standard credit card)
Germany United Kingdom	85 × 55 mm
Australia Brazil Hong Kong Japan Spain	90 × 55 mm
Australia Finland France Israel Norway Russia Spain	90 × 50 mm
Netherlands	74 × 52 mm
Spain	110 × 72 mm

A series

	mm	inches
A0	841 × 1189 (area=1m²)	33⅛ × 46¾
A1	594 × 841	23⅜ × 33⅛
A2	420 × 594	16½ × 33⅛
A3	297 × 420	11¾ × 16½
A4	210 × 297	8¼ × 11¾
A5	148 × 210	5⅞ × 8¼
A6	105 × 148	4⅛ × 5⅞
A7	74 × 105	2⅞ × 4⅛
A8	52 × 74	2 × 2⅞
A9	37 × 52	1½ × 2
A10	26 × 37	1 × 1½

B series

B0	1000 × 1414	39⅜ × 55⅝
B1	707 × 1000	27⅞ × 39⅜
B2	500 × 707	19⅝ × 27⅞
B3	353 × 500	12⅞ × 19⅝
B4	250 × 353	9⅞ × 12⅞
B5	176 × 250	7 × 9⅞
B6	125 × 176	5 × 7
B7	88 × 125	3½ × 5
B8	62 × 88	2½ × 3½
B9	44 × 62	1¾ × 2½
B10	31 × 44	1¼ × 1¾

RA and SRA sizes for printing
R sheets allow for extra trim
SR sheets allow for extra trim and bleed

R A0	860 × 120	33⅞ × 48⅛
R A1	610 × 860	24⅛ × 33⅞
R A2	430 × 610	17 × 24⅛
R A3	305 × 430	12 × 17
R A4	215 × 305	8½ × 12
SR A0	900 × 1280	35½ × 50⅜
SR A1	640 × 900	25¼ × 35½
SR A2	450 × 640	17⅞ × 25¼
SR A3	320 × 450	12⅝ × 17¾
SR A4	225 × 320	8⅞ × 12⅝

Metric C series envelopes

C0	917 × 1297	36⅛ × 51¹/₁₆
C1	648 × 917	25½ × 36⅛
C2	458 × 648	18¹/₁₆ × 33⅛
C3	324 × 458	12¾ × 18¹/₁₆
C4	229 × 324	9 × 12¾
C5	162 × 229	6⅜ × 9
C6	114 × 162	4½ × 6⅜
C7	81 × 114	3³/₁₆ × 4½

Metric special size envelopes

DL	110 × 220	4⁵/₁₆ × 8⅝
C6/5	114 × 229	4½ × 9
C7/6	81 × 162	3³/₁₆ × 6⅜

Aaker, David A., and Erich Joachimsthaler. *Brand Leadership*. New York: The Free Press, 2000.

Blake, George Burroughs, and Nancy Blake-Bohne. *Crafting the Perfect Name: The Art and Science of Naming a Company or Product*. Chicago: Probus Publishing Company, 1991.

Bruce-Mitford, Miranda. *The Illustrated Book of Signs & Symbols*. New York: DK Publishing, Inc., 1996.

Carter, David E. *Branding: The Power of Market Identity*. New York: Hearst Books International, 1999.

Carter, Rob, Ben Day, and Philip Meggs. *Typographic Design: Form and Communication*. New York: John Wiley & Sons, Inc., 1993.

Chermayeff, Ivan, Tom Geismar, and Steff Geissbuhler. *Trademarks Designed by Chermayeff & Geismar*. Basel, Switzerland: Lars Muller Publishers, 2000.

Conway, Lloyd Morgan. *Logo, Identity, Brand, Culture*. Crans-Pres-Celigny, Switzerland: RotoVision SA, 1999.

DeNeve, Rose. *The Designer's Guide to Creating Corporate I.D. Systems*. Cincinnati, OH: North Light Books, 1992.

Eiber, Rick, editor. *World Trademarks: 100 Years, Volumes I and II*. New York: Graphis U.S., Inc., 1996.

Glaser, Milton. *Art Is Work*. Woodstock, NY: The Overlook Press, 2000.

Grant, John. *The New Marketing Manifesto: The 12 Rules for Building Successful Brands in the 21st Century*. London: Texere Publishing Limited, 2000.

"Graphic Design and Advertising Timeline," *Communication Arts* 41, 1 (1999): 80–95.

Heller, Steven. *Paul Rand*. London: Phaidon Press Limited, 1999.

Heller, Steven, and Elinor Pettit. *Graphic Design Time Line: A Century of Design Milestones*. New York: Allworth Press, 2000.

Hill, Sam, and Chris Lederer. *The Infinite Asset: Managing Brands to Build New Value*. Boston: Harvard Business School Press, 2001.

Hine, Thomas. *The Total Package: The Evolution and Secret Meanings of Boxes, Bottles, Cans, and Tubes*. Boston: Little, Brown and Company, 1995.

The History of Printmaking. New York: Scholastic Inc., 1995

Holtzschue, Linda. *Understanding Color: An Introduction for Designers*. New York: John Wiley & Sons, Inc., 2002.

Javed, Naseem. *Naming for Power: Creating Successful Names for the Business World*. New York: Linkbridge Publishing, 1993.

Kerzner, Harold. *Project Management: A Systems Approach to Planning, Scheduling, and Controlling*. New York: Van Nostrand Reinhold, 1989.

Lubliner, Murray J. *Global Corporate Identity: The Cross-Border Marketing Challenge*. Rockport, MA: Rockport Publishers, Inc., 1994.

Man, John. *Alpha Beta: How Our Alphabet Shaped the Western World*. London: Headlline Book Publishing, 2000.

Meggs, Philip B. *A History of Graphic Design*. New York: John Wiley & Sons, Inc., 1998.

Mollerup, Per. *Marks of Excellence: The History and Taxonomy of Trademarks*. London: Phaidon Press Limited, 1997.

Napoles, Veronica. *Corporate Identity Design*. New York: John Wiley & Sons, Inc., 1988.

Olins, Wally. *Corporate Identity: Making Business Strategy Visible Through Design*. Boston: Harvard Business School Press, 1989.

Paos, editor. *New Decomas: Design Conscious Management Strategy.* Seoul: Design House Inc., 1994.

Pavitt, Jane, editor. *Brand New.* London: V&A Publications, 2000.

Remington, R. Roger. *Lester Beall: Trailblazer of American Graphic Design.* New York: W. W. Norton & Company, 1996.

Ries, Al, and Jack Trout. *Positioning: The Battle for Your Mind.* New York: Warner Books, Inc., 1986.

Rogener, Stefan, Albert-Jan Pool, and Ursula Packhauser. *Branding with Type: How Type Sells.* Mountain View, CA: Adobe Press, 1995.

Sharp, Harold S. *Advertising Slogans of America.* Metuchen, NJ: The Scarecrow Press, Inc., 1984.

Spiekerman, Erik, and E. M. Ginger. *Stop Stealing Sheep & Find Out How Type Works.* Mountain View, CA: Adobe Press, 1993.

Sweet, Fay. *MetaDesign: Design from the World Up.* New York: Watson-Guptill Publications, 1999.

Traverso, Debra Koontz. *Outsmarting Goliath: How to Achieve Equal Footing with Companies That are Bigger, Richer, Older, and Better Known.* Princeton, NJ: Bloomberg Press, 2000.

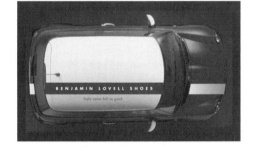

Benjamin Lovell Shoes' Mini Cooper designed by Thom & Dave